Lawrence L. and Eda J. LeShan

I0410472

PATRIOTISM
FOR GROWNUPS

HOW TO BE A CITIZEN IN THE 21ST CENTURY

TRAFFORD

Note for Librarians: A cataloguing record for this book is available from Library and Archives Canada at www.collectionscanada.ca/amicus/index-e.html

ISBN 1-4120-5665-9

Printed on chlorine/bleach free, 100% recycled paper. Trafford's print shop runs on "green energy" from solar, wind and other environmentally-friendly power sources.

TRAFFORD

Offices in Canada, USA, Ireland and UK
This book was published *on-demand* in cooperation with Trafford Publishing. On-demand publishing is a unique process and service of making a book available for retail sale to the public taking advantage of on-demand manufacturing and Internet marketing. On-demand publishing includes promotions, retail sales, manufacturing, order fulfilment, accounting and collecting royalties on behalf of the author.

Book sales for North America and international:
Trafford Publishing, 6E–2333 Government St.,
Victoria, BC v8t 4p4 CANADA
phone 250 383 6864 (toll-free 1 888 232 4444)
fax 250 383 6804; email to orders@trafford.com
Book sales in Europe:
Trafford Publishing (uk) Ltd., Enterprise House, Wistaston Road Business Centre,
Wistaston Road, Crewe, Cheshire cw2 7rp UNITED KINGDOM
phone 01270 251 396 (local rate 0845 230 9601)
facsimile 01270 254 983; orders.uk@trafford.com
Order online at:
trafford.com/05-0563

10 9 8 7 6 5 4 3 2

Other Books by Eda LeShan…

THEATRE PLAYS

The Lobster Reef
Time Enough for Love
Waiting for Sylvia
The Gardener

Other Books by Lawrence LeShan…

Counseling the Dying (with Bowers, Jackson and Knight)
The Medium, the Mystic and the Physicist
How to Meditate
Alternative Realities
You Can Fight For Your Life:
Emotional Factors in the Development of Cancer
Einstein's Space and Van Gogh's Sky
(with Henry Margenau)
The Mechanic and the Gardener:
Understanding the Wholistic Revolution in Medicine
The World of the Paranormal: The Next Frontier
Cancer as a Turning Point
The Dilemma of Psychology
The Psychology of War
Meditating to Attain a Healthy Body Weight
Beyond Technique:
Bringing Psychotherapy into the 21st Century
An Ethic for the Age of Space:
A Touchstone for Life Among the Stars

Dedicated to
Our daughter, Wendy, of whom we are very proud.

and with respect and gratitude to
Andrew Goodman, James Chaney
and Michael Schwerner.

TABLE OF CONTENTS

CHAPTER 1

A WINDOW OF OPPORTUNITY

IN THE LONG, SLOW DEVELOPMENT of the human race our progress has been marked by three sharp, definitive steps carried out by major governments. All three initially failed to lead to successful acceptance or action. Little attention was paid to them by large segments of the human population and their implications were generally ignored.

And yet they were there. And behind them a movement of critical importance for us today.

The first was a Papal Bull, *Sublimis Deus*, issued in 1537, a period in which the Vatican was a strong secular as well as religious authority. It stated that all human beings had souls, the color of their skin or the origin of their forefathers notwithstanding. This was the first major recognition of the intrinsic unity of the human race, that differences are essentially minor, and that we all belong to the same family. This, immensely-revolutionary-at-the-time, statement is one whose implications we are still only slowly accepting, although it undoubtedly contributed to the fact that, generally speaking, slavery ended earlier in countries with predominantly Catholic populations than in those which were predominantly Protestant.

The second great governmentally-sponsored step in our development occurred in 1993 when, for the first time in human history, a major political power mobilized its army and sent it abroad with just one purpose—to feed starving people. There was nothing in Somalia that the United States wanted. There was no oil, no possibility of political gain nor anything but sand and hunger.

The expedition itself was a failure. The United States army was ill prepared to deal effectively with a disorganized society of the kind which we found there. Failure it was, but the fact that the attempt was made with its implied statement that all human beings carry responsibility for the lives of all others was a tremendous event and success. It was a major step forward in our slow march toward human adulthood.

In a slightly later example of this step, in the acceptance speech for the 1988 Nobel Peace Prize, Javier Perez De Cuellar (representing the United Nations Peace-Keeping forces) said:

The technique which has come to be called peacekeeping uses soldiers as the servants of peace rather than as the instruments of war. It introduces to the military sphere the principle of nonviolence.

Never before in history have military forces been employed internationally not to wage war, not to establish domination, and not to serve the interests of any power or group of powers, but rather to prevent conflict between people.

The third step was at Kyoto in the year 2000 where a majority of the nations of the world declared that all human beings bear responsibility for the safety and ecology of our only planet and for maintaining a livable environment for our children.

Here, as in the previous steps, there were many who were not yet ready to make the statement. To our shame, the United States government rejected it. Again it was a revolutionary development, inconceivable in the past, and a mark of our slow, irregular, terribly uneven progress.[1]

The rejection of each of the three steps has generally been in the name of patriotism. We have always held, and still hold it true, that loyalty to something larger than oneself is a high virtue and a mark of an admirable person. We regard the person without it as paltry at best. We expect others and ourselves to put a strong value on loyalty to a group, and if the object of our loyalty is threatened to stand, fight and, if necessary, die for it. What we often forget is that in different historical periods our loyalty has been to different **size** groups. First was the family, then the clan, the tribe, the province, and now the nation. In each period the prevailing patriotism was at least as strong and exclusive as it is today towards a nation. Albert Schweitzer wrote in the *Saturday Review of Literature* in 1953:

> *For the primitive the circle of solidarity is restricted. It is limited…to the members of his tribe….In my hospital I have primitives. When I have occasion to ask a patient of this category to render some small service to a bed-ridden fellow patient, he will oblige only if the latter belongs to his tribe. If this is not*

the case he will reply quite candidly "This is not brother for me." No amount of persuasion and no kind of threat will budge his from his refusal to do the unimaginable thing: putting himself out for a stranger. I am the one who has to give in.

There are two reasons why today we consider this kind of loyalty to a group a **primitive** kind of patriotism. First because it is loyalty to a group much smaller than the one toward which we are patriotic, second because it is so complete, compelling and exclusive. We have progressed to the degree that when a fellow human being is in trouble, is drowning, or is ill or dying and we are nearby, his or her suffering makes us go beyond the idea that all human beings are critically defined by their belonging to one nation or to another. For us, if the person in the next hospital bed needs a drink of water he is no longer defined as an American or a Frenchman, Black, Brown, White, Yellow or Red. He is a fellow mortal.

But today, outside of such special circumstances, we are mostly patriots with loyalty to a nation. In the last few centuries this is the size group towards which our identification and loyalty has evolved. And slowly we are moving beyond this as shown by the Papal Bull of 1537, by Somalia, by Kyoto, and by our behavior toward the sick person in the next bed.

Loyalty to a tribe, a city or a province was outgrown and changed by the course of human events and by new ideas and new technologies. The invention of the cannon and later of double entry bookkeeping made loyalty to a city obsolete. Patriotism only to a nation is now outworn. A virus, whether genetically tailored or spontaneous mutation, or a radioactive cloud acts as if political boundaries were non-existent. Not a customs office, a Maginot Line or a Berlin Wall presents the slightest obstacle to them. In the middle of the Pacific, with no other ships or land in sight for weeks at a time, Thor Heyerdahyl, close to the surface of the water in his reed-constructed Kon Tiki, found the ocean contaminated by oil droplets from tankers thousands of miles away as they flushed out their tanks. Before the era of international terrorism we have learned that all national borders are so porous that no government can prevent the flow of illicit drugs across them. The time of the nation state being the group to which we give our loyalty is rapidly passing. We humans are ready for the next step.

It should be obvious that our loyalty to a larger group does not lessen our loyalty, our love and concern for the smaller one. More loyalty to our country does not make less loyalty to our family. Increasing the size of the object of our patriotism, our loyalty, increases the amount of it. Shakespeare wrote that love "grows by its own increase." The same thing is true of patriotism.

The best way to reinforce and strengthen an entity is to enclose it as an integral part of a larger one. Ask yourself if Iowa or Delaware or Texas would be stronger and living in them would be better if there were fifty individual countries instead of one United States in which they are embedded. Would your family be better off if you lived in an independent Brittany, South Carolina or Venice than if you lived in France, the United States or Italy. Every country that joined the United Nations was stating clearly that membership in a larger whole was good for their country and that they were joining for patriotic reasons.

In the first quarter of the 20th Century psychologists in the "Gestalt" school studied the relationship of the part to the whole. Their conclusion was that membership in the larger picture strengthens and clarifies the part. The entity that is part of a pattern is made sharper and stronger by its participation in the larger pattern. If my patriotism to my own country impels me to a concern with the ecology in which its citizens, my family and I live, I can only strengthen that ecology by concern with the ecology of the whole world. That was the specific lesson of Kyoto.

We do not know what laws govern our choice of the size of the group to which we are loyal. We are not clear on why in wartime we enlist in the army as "Americans" or "Frenchmen," but in combat we fight for far different size groups than these. As innumerable memoirs and studies have shown (ranging from "All Quiet on the Western Front" to the United States Army's intensive and extensive study "Why Men Fight") in combat we fight for "Third Squad" or "Charlie Company," but not for the "22nd Regiment," the "4th Division," "3rd Army," or for "France" or "The United States." We are, if we are sports fans, loyal to "The Yankees" or "The Red Sox," but not "The American League" or "The National League."

Although we do not know what laws govern such choices, we do know that, in peacetime at least, the crucial factors governing our choices include what we are taught as children and the examples of our parents and other adult teachers. We do know that steps from a smaller loyalty group to a larger one can and have been made. After Garibaldi there was much less exclusive loyalty to "Milan" or "Genoa" and much more to "Italy." The same is true of "Hesse," "Bavaria" and "Germany" after Bismarck. "Burgundians" and "Normans" became "Frenchmen." In the United States "Vermonters" and "Virginians" became "Americans." Further we know that we are getting ready for the next step and that many individuals are actually making it. There has been, for example, a growing spate of organizations which are dedicated to working in this direction. There is, for example, *Medicine Sans Frontiers*, the Environmental Defense Fund, Greenpeace, Habitat for Humanity, student exchange and work programs, The Peace Corps. Each of us could think of others. The fact that these organizations are household words today shows that a larger change than we have been aware of is slowly, and with much irregularity and back-and-forthing, taking place.

We are beginning to see the whole Earth, that beautiful blue marble hanging in space, as a single, fragile entity.

This is a time of opportunity. For the first time in history all the peoples on Earth have a common present. No longer does news of what is happening on the other side of the globe come to us irregularly and with great delay. Each nation is now the immediate neighbor of every other. Literally we see what happens as it happens or a fraction of a second later. The immediacy of our observation is limited only by the speed of light. The rate at which we can and do change has been increasing almost as rapidly as has been the ease and speed of communication between individuals and groups. It is possible for us to also accelerate our growth toward human adulthood. We can speed the development of our patriotism, our loyalty, to the next stage where it will be to the entire human race, and this includes making sure there is a survivable environment for our children and their children.

Each generation teaches the meaning of patriotism to its children. We do this primarily by example. Social attitudes, like a cold, can not be taught. They must be caught. If we lead, our children will follow. They are more ready than we know. Now, when from an early age they play across all borders with the internet and are psychologically ready to move beyond our present definition of patriotism, we have the wonderful opportunity to move ahead of where we are now and take our species to new heights. It only takes the vision and the will.

ENDNOTES

---

[1] There have been other steps on the road to the adulthood of our species. All *were* real steps even though they each ran into tremendous opposition by groups that believed they violated things like "self determination of nations," "property rights," or free this or that. In 1948 the United Nations passed The Universal Declaration of Human Rights. This states that every citizen of every nation has the right to life, liberty, freedom from personal attack, from slavery, and torture, has a right under law to be presumed innocent until proven guilty, has the right to privacy, and the expression of conscience and religion. All through human history until a few hundred years ago this statement would have been greeted with, at best, a blank stare and amazed laughter.

Indeed, we might list a fifth step of the same size as these others, the right of species other than our own to exist on their own natural territories was recognized by a nation. This is a statement by a major government that human beings are an integral part of the great pattern of biodiversity that exists on our planet and of which we are a part. It does not say that we should preserve other species in our zoos for our own profit or amusement. It is a statement of a dawning recognition that we are no longer only Floridians or Welshmen, no longer just Frenchmen or Italians, but we are members of a species that can no longer be seen as legitimate with a full right to exist as long as other species are not also recognized as legitimate with an equal right.

We are gradually realizing that the entire world is a nest which we share with others and that we foul at our peril. The death of another species, irrecoverable, final and forever, diminishes us in ways we do not begin to comprehend. It would, we know, be sad to live in a world without whales, but, deep down, we also know that losing the spotted owl or the lynx would also make us less. We are beginning to sense that when another species with which we share our earth home become extinct, life not only becomes somehow less joyful but we ourselves somehow move higher on the endangered species list.

CHAPTER 2

ACTION TO MAKE
A DIFFERENCE

IT IS A PROFOUND fallacy to believe that we can change the way that the world acts without first changing the way that we ourselves act. During the 1960s that superb child psychiatrist Fritz Redl was lecturing to a group of young parents. One of them asked him, "How can we raise children so that they will act with integrity and have concern for others in a materialistic age when baseball players, presidents of large companies, politicians and other leaders are so corrupt and selfish?" Redl answered, "There are three things you can do to accomplish this. I want you all to write them down." All of us immediately poised our pencils. Redl then said, "The three things are example, example, example!"

There are a great many things that we each can do in order to encourage our children and others around us to develop a concern and loyalty to the entire human race and to the delicate balances of our only and lovely planet. I will mention only a few of them here. Once we ourselves are oriented in this direction, others will constantly occurs to us. These are things that we can do without changing our entire lives. They are typical of the little steps we can make which can make a great difference. Eleanor Roosevelt said, "It is better to light one candle than to curse the darkness." It is not only true that when we light one candle we lessen the darkness if only by a small amount. It is also an example to others and if we provide enough examples some will be followed and some of them will be followed until we will have a blazing sun. Health is just as infectious as disease—steps in the right direction are followed as much as steps in the wrong one.

Very often an action seems to have no direct effect and we become discouraged, not realizing that what we have done adds our tiny amount of pressure helping us move toward the next step. We are in a process in our culture of growing toward a patriotism in which the entire human race is the "in-group" and in which all of us and our children and their children are an object of our loyalty. This sounds overwhelming, but it is no larger than the previous steps from the family to the clan and ultimately to the nation. And as examples, we might look at each of the three "Flower Children" movements in Western history—each of which was carried out by a comparatively small group, each of which was in the teeth of established opinion, each of which was strongly attacked and its members often brutalized and each of which was successful and attained its goal.

The first was the Cathars in southern France in the 14th Century. They were deeply religious, but rejected the hierarchy of the Catholic Church because of its hypocrisy and corruption. They prayed in woods and fields instead of the churches, established communes (one of which survived in the Pyrenees until Napoleon's army wiped it out five hundred years later.) They invented the revolutionary idea of protection of the weak "Women and children to the lifeboats first" and the equally revolutionary idea that love was the natural basis for marriage. They fomented university revolutions all over Europe. Because of their refusal to obey the Vatican, the Fourth Crusade was called against them and they were nearly all killed as heretics.

But their ideas and beliefs kept circulating and ultimately were the foundation of the very basic reforms of the Catholic Church, the Protestant Revolution and finally after a long struggle to the freedom of religion we have today.

The second "Flower Children" movement was the group in and around Boston in the years before the Civil War. They often lived in the woods, spent a few years with the Gypsies, bummed around Europe, met in Margaret Fuller's coffee house (William James called her "the wickedest woman in New England!") and generally annoyed the establishment no end. Some of them (for example, Thoreau, Emerson, Hawthorne) have now been lionized. Their basic belief was that slavery was wrong. Not having draft cards to burn—as did the next group of Flower Children—they burned copies of the Constitution in Scollay Square to protest government support for slavery. The country was scandalized. The flower children were outraged about slavery and ultimately made it a moral issue for the

rest of the country. Once that had happened, the end
of slavery was inexorable.

The third group was that of our Flower Children
of the 1960s. They had two basic beliefs. One was that
the Vietnam War was an evil that should be ended.
The second was that racial discrimination was wrong
and must be stopped. Their actions led to the ending
of our war in Vietnam. They also succeeded in making
racial discrimination a moral issue and, although it is
far from being ended in the United States, its eventual
end is inevitable.

These are larger social movements which we
can see in historical perspective. Just as important,
however, are the small and everyday actions we can
take without disrupting our lives or our immediate
responsibilities. As I list below a few of these, they
will seem familiar and unimportant. And yet they
are the crucial and central things that each of us can
do to help human loyalty and patriotism change to
something more inclusive of all of us, now and in the
future.

An election is approaching, whether for City
Council in your area or for President of your country.
Check out each candidate. You (or your children)
can obtain their voting records from the internet.
Organizations such as Greenpeace or The League of
Women Voters or many others can help you evaluate
them. Is this candidate primarily concerned with her
career or with our deepest goals for the human race?
Does he ever "vote his conscience?" Is the concern
with votes and what we seem to want now or with our
children and the globe on which we live? If he or she is
running for or is likely to go on to high office, will we

then be likely to have a politician or a statesman?

Write up the results of your investigation of each candidate (or take the evaluations of one of the serious ecology organizations) and Xerox some copies. Put them up on local bulletin boards. You and your spouse or partner and your kids can spend a few hours putting them in local mailboxes. In this you are not only working for the best (from your point of view) candidate regardless of slogans or party, you are advocating a point of view about what is important in deciding for whom to vote.

And after evaluation and discussion—Vote! and bring your children with you to this most sacred of our political activities. Many places to vote are in the basement of a school or a church, but wherever they are, and however informal and crowded or empty, they are holy ground. Be aware of this and make sure that your children are also.

A mom-and-pop stationery store in your neighborhood has given up selling tobacco because they do not believe in selling things that are bad for people's health. Shop there instead of the big chain across the street even if the chain can sell at a slightly lower price. Let your children and your friends and neighbors know that you are doing this and why. To encourage and to help to survive the people on our side is valuable action toward attaining movement in the direction we wish to go.

You are considering buying a car. Check out the ecology factors and get the entire family involved. Buy according to these and write the maker of your new possession why you bought it. (Companies are influenced by letters of this sort.) When you hear your children boasting to their friends that "Our car has a lower poison emission rate than yours and also gets better gas mileage" you will know that you have started a powerful ripple effect. If you are more concerned with ecology factors than in size or advertising cleverness and you have gotten your children, and perhaps your friends, involved in the process of choice, they will tend to follow your lead as to primary concern and loyalty.

There are serious organizations devoted to promoting patriotism to the entire human race and to the ecology now and in the future. The Sierra Club (www.sierraclub.org) may well be "Grandma" of these organizations and still is an outstanding example, but there are now also many others, each with a slightly different focus. There is the World Wildlife Fund, The Environmental Defense League, Greenpeace, Save the Children Federation, Zero Population Growth, Amnesty International, Earth Justice, The Wilderness Society, The Natural Resources Defense Council, The Nature Conservancy, and the list goes on. Find out about these. (Your local librarian will be glad to help and the internet is another source.) Check them out. Which one appeals to you the most? How much of the money raised goes to "administrative costs" and how large a percentage to the actual work? (A minimum of 80% of total income should go to the actual work. Some, like The Sierra Club, will be more.) Join the ones you like most after this search. Read their publication which will be sent to you when you become a member. A paid-up membership card makes a wonderful gift especially for "the person who has everything." The gift will not be one that they use once and then forget.

They will be reminded every time the organization's publication arrives. (And they will find themselves on the advertising list of other organizations of the same kind!) It will also make a good gift for local, state and federal officials, school libraries and those people on your Christmas list to whom you formerly gave ties, gloves and assorted white elephants.

When you are buying a wide variety of things such as lawn fertilizer or cleansers of different types, check on how biodegradable they are. (A good way to compare companies, their products and policies, is to use such sites as www.responsibleshopper.com.) Better yet, see if the High School Chemistry teacher will make doing this a class project. And look for those products which *never* decay (for example, the plastic connectors that are often on six packs of beer and soft drinks which seem guaranteed to last for forty or fifty generations and be a deadly trap for ducks and some small mammals). Make what you find in your (or your children's) research a major factor in deciding what you buy. Let the companies know why you are rejecting their product.

If you belong to an organization such as the Rotary Club, the Elks, or the American Legion, the local chapter is often a good base from which to act

If you can get on the local school board, or establish some influence there, there is an obvious and very large number of things you can work for. A required class in high school civics, for example with a class project of the leading needs of the community and which government structures are most responsible in the specific area of the needs. Social science credits for community service are being issued in an increasing number of schools. Can yours add to the list? (A number of possibilities of this sort which have been put in operation successfully in a number of schools are described in Chapter 7.)

Christmas is a wonderful opportunity to work for a wider patriotism. It is a good time for children to raise money for UNICEF and for deprived children everywhere. And observe how this kind of action changes and improves children's feelings about Christmas and about themselves.

Once you begin to look in this direction you will find that you are not alone, that there are more organizations in your area working toward a wider concern and patriotism than you were probably aware of. Nearly all need volunteers. (All need money!) Is there a branch of "The Fortune Society" trying to help ex-convicts who want to turn their lives around in your neighborhood? You can reach Amnesty International and help work against political injustice everywhere with one telephone call or e-mail. Is there a branch of "God's Love, We Deliver" preparing and delivering food to housebound AIDS and other patients? Is there a "Big Brother" or "Big Sister" or "Boys and Girls Club?" Is there a meeting house of The Society of Friends or a local chapter of the Society for Ethical Culture in your area? You will find either of these actively engaged in local, national and international projects. Is there a "We Harvest" organization collecting food from restaurants and bringing it to public soup kitchens? And the list goes from *Medicins Sans Frontieres* to The World Wildlife Fund to Meals on Wheels. Getting involved in any of these (and, if you have any kids getting *them* involved) teaches our children three lessons. First, that adults care enough about them to work for their safety now and in the future. Second, that they can make a difference, that they have "environmental competence." Third, how to be citizens of the world as well as of their own country, that the object of their patriotism can be the human race as well as to the nation in which they live.

We have listed here a few of the things that one can do without making a major change in one's life. These are evolutionary changes in the direction we wish to go, not revolutionary ones. Revolutions are notoriously unstable and often produce effects opposite to those we are seeking. The idealistic French Revolution produced Napoleon; the equally idealistic Russian one produced Stalin. Further, making a revolution often demands a complete change in one's life patterns. Most of us have responsibilities which we could not fulfill if we enlisted in a revolutionary action group. There are times in human history when this has been necessary, when it was the best and apparently only solution to a terrible political situation, but this is not true now. One only, to use the old phrase, "goes to the barricades" in times of great disaster, dictatorship and emergency. Mostly, as now, there are better ways.

Another way of approaching this area was written by one of us (EJL) for her column in Newsday "Life Over Sixty" and reprinted in her book *It's Better to be Over the Hill Than Under It* (Newmarket Press, New York 1990).

ONE PERSON MAKES A DIFFERENCE

Author Jo Coudert, whom I have loved for many years because of her fantastic book Advice From a Failure

(Scarborough House, 1983) wrote an article for Woman's Day (December 19, 1989) called "I'm a Bag Lady for the World." In it she tells of loving to take walks in the semi-rural area where she lives but finding it essential, despite its interfering with a beloved activity, to stop along the way and pick up other people's garbage.

She and I are soulmates. When I had a house on Cape Cod I took a plastic bag with me whenever I went for a walk, and collected beer cans, soda bottles, and McDonald's wrappings along the way. I was furious at the people who had so little concern for their planet but I figured bending so much was good for me. Ms. Coudert decided more recently that she would become "a fool for the world." She writes, "We've finally come to understand that the world is our home—that an oil spill thousands of miles away is in our front yards, that the greenhouse effect warms us all, that it is our water being polluted, our food adulterated…. We also feel helpless to do much about it." She quotes Shirley Temple Black (that adorable curly-head has turned out pretty well!) who said, "Think globally, act locally."

I get a lot of sad mail from people who are handicapped by old age or specific disabilities. They say that their lives are useless and meaningless, that they have nothing to do. Others, healthy and whole, write of loneliness, of not feeling needed by grown children.

In the city of New York, I feel essential at least to my neighborhood because I pick up all the garbage I pass and take it to the next trash can I pass. I write furious letters to congressmen and department heads about black smoke coming out of chimneys and places where the Sanitation Department doesn't go because the people are too poor and discouraged to fight City Hall.

We have no business complaining that we are not

useful and that nobody needs us. The world needs every ounce of strength left in our bodies to fight the disasters we could never have imagined when we were young.

Many of the young activists of the sixties became very discouraged about not having the power to change society; I, however, feel they did PLENTY by helping to end a terrible war. However, now what many of these "flower children" in their late thirties and forties say is that they have learned the power of individual action. A Wall Street banker gives two evenings a week working in a shelter for the homeless; two young women walk the streets of their town with hot coffee and sandwiches for families sleeping in cars and people hidden in the shadows of store entrances. One young woman organized a letter campaign for better streetlights and got them.

Old age is no excuse for copping out. Each of us can find ways in which to make a difference. I got a letter from the daughter of a woman with terminal cancer who had inserted a letter in her will that she did not want life-support systems used when her life as a real person was over. Several months before she died, she told her daughter, "Listen, just before you pull the plug, I want you to send this money to Greenpeace in my memory," and handed her daughter a fifty-dollar bill.

Each step forward is worth taking even though it does not seem to have an immediate effect or even when it seems to be a failure. In 1944 we were living in the town of Martinsburg, West Virginia as LLL was stationed at a nearby Army hospital. The town was completely segregated down to the water fountains and the seats on the buses. There was no place outside of the church where African-Americans could meet in groups. Further there was no place for young people of either race to meet. As one young White boy put it, "In the Summer we can get together at the movies or in the bushes. In the Winter there is only the movies and we don't have the money for them very often."

A teenage canteen was clearly badly needed. In her capacity as Child Welfare Worker for the county (and three adjoining ones) EJL decided to try to organize the building of one. It became immediately clear that this could only be done if it were a "Whites Only" place and this was against our principles. But the need was there. We went to Mr. Raymer, the head of the African-American community, for advice. (At his request and for our own safety going to his house after dark and parking several blocks away!) He suggested that we work for a white teenage canteen *and* a Black Social Center which would include a young people's canteen. We organized the "Martinsburg Interracial Council" and at the end of about a year both canteen and social center were functioning, albeit on a completely segregated basis.

This was not accomplished without difficulty and without both pleasant and unpleasant surprises. Fortunately EJL had established a relationship with the local Police Chief in her capacity as Child Welfare Worker. Thus, when things had become particularly unpleasant at night, there began to be frequent drive-bys by the patrol cars and the word went out from the Chief. The 2 a.m. loud horn honkings under the window, the broken windshields, the nightly stones thrown at the windows and slashed tires on our car and the obscene telephone calls and threats became less frequent. When the Mayor of Martinsburg went to the Army hospital and asked to have LLL transferred because "He and his wife are such troublemakers and keep trying to bring all that Red equality stuff into town" he was listened to very politely by the Regular Army head of the hospital, Colonel Cook. After the Mayor finished, Cook told him that he understood his problem and sympathized with him. To show his sympathy he would advise the Interracial Council to hold a public meeting and he would tell his Chief of Psychiatry to speak at it on the subject of "The Neurotic Bases of Race Prejudice," and that if there was any disturbance at the meeting he, Colonel Cook, would look again at the hospital policy of hiring local people as civilian aides and see how many such jobs he could do without or replace with Army personnel.

Some time later the Army transferred LLL elsewhere. The members of the Interracial Council decided that without the support of the two of us it was no longer safe to continue and dissolved the organization. We were sad and disheartened that there would be no base for continued social action in the town.

However, when the new federal laws against segregation came into effect a few years later, Martinsburg was the first town in the state to follow them.

Fifty years later we returned to Martinsburg. As we drove down Main Street we saw, coming towards us, the children and teachers of a nursery school. They came two by two holding hands. They were completely mixed, White faces and Black faces. One teacher was White, the other was not. We looked at each other as they passed and both of us broke into tears. Our Interracial Council may have long since dissolved, but the tiny actions we had made had joined with the work and examples of many, many others and here was the result walking down Main Street.

It is not easy to act and to try to make things better. We all have large emotional investments in the Status Quo and there is a general feeling that it is better to let things go on as they are rather than to upset things and that changes lead to more changes and to God knows where after that. Generally speaking when people say to you "Be realistic" they really mean "Be cynical about human beings and salve your conscience about doing nothing by concluding that nothing can be done." This teaches you to stifle the action arising from indignation, just anger and compassion and not have any of these emotions and to tiptoe as safely as you can through your life and toward your death.

CHAPTER 3

AN OMBUDSMAN
FOR OUR CHILDREN

WATCH A CHILD ON the street who has just learned to walk. How proud and happy and exploratory she is. Look at a baby in a carriage. Look at a three-year-old eating in a restaurant with his family. Wave to a four-year-old in her father's arms. Smile at a six-year-old with his mother on a bus.

Most of us, at these moments, if we look within, find a feeling of "That's what it's all about. That's what's really important."

This feeling reflects a deep truth. The first law of biology is "Any species which does not protect its young becomes extinct." Protection, of course, comes in many forms, from carrying one offspring in a secure pouch to making so many offspring that some will survive—a sort of statistical protection.

The human way is to love and protect and teach one or a very small group at a time. Each one is reacted to as precious. The human need for this is so great that if infants are not sufficiently held and touched and loved they suffer deep damage to their development.

Unfortunately there are many adults who can not express their need to love and protect children. For some this is true because of damage that they themselves suffered in their development, some because of economic and/or overwhelming cultural imperatives. A large percentage of human children grow up with their basic need to be touched, held and loved unfulfilled.

An important part of the new patriotism is that we care and protect not only our biological and legally adopted children, but all children, for each patriotic adult to be a part-time ombudsman for all children everywhere.

This is an overwhelming idea. It is too large a burden. We can not shoulder it no matter how much we wish that we could. How can I act on it? Where do I choose to put my ounces of strength against the tremendous worldwide need of children? How can I act to fulfil the role of ombudsman?

There are so many choices. There are, for examples, organizations such as Save the Children in which you can help a specific child who is now starving somewhere on Earth. You provide the monetary pittance necessary for basic food, medicine and schooling (generally about the same monthly cost as an evening at the movies for you and your family) and exchange letters and photographs with the child. There are more general child help organizations ranging from UNICEF to The Police Athletic League. There are religious groups such as Catholic Charities which will accept funds earmarked for children. There is the American Jewish

World Service which specializes in children caught in the pandemic of AIDS in sub-Saharan Africa. And many others. You can keep a special eye on laws, both local and national, which affect children and do whatever lobbying you can. In your neighborhood volunteers are needed by organizations such as "Big Brothers," "Big Sisters" and "Boys and Girls Clubs." Even if you yourself are housebound you can arrange with the local school system to have students sent to you for special tutoring in subjects in which they are now struggling unsuccessfully.

All of these, and many more are ways of expressing grownup patriotism and all are very likely to be personally rewarding to you yourself. But how do you choose?

An answer to this question may lie in an old legend. In the Bible, in Psalm 56, we are told that "God preserves all your tears." The legend which attempts to explain this strange sentence and say why God would do this is as follows: When you arrive in Heaven you are confused and do not know how to behave. You are given a bottle which contains the water in all the tears you shed while you lived on Earth. The task which goes with this gift is that you yourself must search for and find the best possible use for this one little bottle of purified liquid.

Somewhere in a desert, a few inches under the surface, is a seed. It has been there a long time and, in spite of its hard shell, is slowly drying out to its heart. Soon it will die. With a little water it could send out tendrils to the deep water table beneath it and develop into a strong hardy plant and send out shoots until the entire barren area of the desert is in bloom and provides nourishment for the desert animals and nomads.

Somewhere on Earth there is a person, alone in a room who has been badly burned and desperately needs liquid to cool the scorched flesh. Somewhere there is a child who is dying of thirst in an empty house. There is a man on a raft lost at sea with his lips black from lack of drinkable liquid. There is a woman who can not nurse her starving baby because of lack of water. You find many, many lacks like these. Your task is to search the entire world until you find the one to whom you wish to give the one small bottle of water you have. After you have completed the task and brought back the empty bottle, you find that you now know how to behave in Heaven.

The answer to the problem of what action one person can take in view of the tremendous needs of children the world over is that you, as a unique individual, choose the one need that most fills you with indignation and compassion and act there. There are very many strong needs, if we do not see them it is because we prefer not to. Any one you choose will not only express your patriotism, it will almost certainly be both personally rewarding and fulfilling. If you involve your children and/or your friends in it also it will help set up the ripple effect that widens both the action and the effects.

Wherever you choose to put your efforts toward the betterment of the human race, now or in the future, one thing you can be certain of. No forward movement is isolated. In Barry Commoner's "Four Laws of Ecology" the first law is "Everything is connected to everything else." Helping to feed starving people in

Africa has a wider effect than just the survival of the individuals. Starving people destroy their environment in their desperation. The African paleo-anthropologist Richard Leakey wrote somewhere, "It takes at least one square meal a day to be an environmentalist." Further it sets an example for others. And binds us a little bit closer as members of the same family.

It is amazing and saddening how many of us are afraid of giving our sense of compassion and our love acceptance and expression. We are mostly afraid that it will sweep us away and overwhelm us, that it will lead to pain we fear we can not bear.

To be truthful, both love *and* compassion are dangerous. They can cause us pain as well as joy and fulfillment. But we need them to develop as full human beings as much as a garden needs water. If there is no water the garden can not grow and become. There is no danger on the barren grounds of the winds of time and chance damaging the growing shoots, the hopeful buds and the blooming plants. Yet, given these two choices, which would we prefer our gardens and life to be?

In 1980 and 1981 one of us (EJL) had a regular column on CBS Radio called "Getting Along." There were a great many requests for transcripts of the talks. The one that received the most requests is this one.

THE MOST ENDANGERED SPECIES

I love to watch such television programs as "Wild Kingdom," where I can get an appreciation of all the beautiful and fascinating animals there are in the world— and I worry terribly about the fact that so many of them are on the way to extinction. But there is one endangered species that I worry about all the time.

The most endangered species on earth are human children. What we need to do it take over one of our National Parks, put fences all around it, and try to raise human children in an environment that would save the species. I would want this park to be at least a thousand miles away from the nearest nuclear plant. The water the children drank would have to come from some spring having its origin somewhere near the North Pole so it couldn't be contaminated. The soil would have to be tested before a vegetable garden could be planted, to make sure there hadn't been any seepage from industrial plants or the use of insect sprays or chemical fertilizers. A canopy would have to be built over the entire park so that acid rain couldn't fall into the ponds and lakes.

There is no place on earth anymore where we could guarantee such environmental safety, but let's pursue this process of saving the species, anyway.

All the mothers in this park would be given medical care and the best possible nutrition. With all the money we are now going to save by not providing vitamins and milk to the pregnant poor in our cities, we could certainly provide such things for this small group in the park. We will be saving so much money on everyone else's prenatal and infant nutrition and on medical care that the kids in the park will be able to have all the things that will make them grow up strong and intelligent and healthy. We'll give them the hot lunches we've taken out of the schools, and of course there will be good teachers and small classes and plenty of recreational programs, and special education for their parents, so they can have a happy home life.

Then we can take all the books from the libraries we are closing, and all the ballet companies and orchestras we are no longer funding, and send them all to the park so the children can have a rich cultural experience. And finally, all the professors from all the colleges that will have to close because of cuts in student loans can be sent to the park so that every child can have a college education.

The nice thing about my plan is that these wonderful children would be so smart and so healthy and so responsible that they'd probably run away from the park when they were grown up and would try to save whatever was left of the rest of the other children. I hope it won't be too late.

(Reprinted in *Living Your Life*, Harper & Row, 1982.)

CHAPTER 4

LOYALTY TO THE PRESENT AND THE FUTURE

WE HUMAN BEINGS HAVE always felt that loyalty to a group larger than oneself was an important virtue and that a person without it was a very poor specimen of our species. Sir Walter Scott expressed this dramatically (and more strongly than most of us would accept) but nevertheless stated clearly our present view of patriotism.

PATRIOTISM

Breathes there the man with soul so dead,
Who never to himself hath said,
"This is my own, my native land!"
Whose heart hath ne'er within him burn'd
As home his footsteps he hath turn'd
 From wandering on a foreign strand?
If such there breathe, go, mark him well;
For him no minstrel raptures swell;
High though his titles, proud his name,

41

Boundless his wealth as wish can claim;
Despite those titles, power, and pelf,
The wretch, concentred all in self,
Living, shall forfeit all renown,
And doubly dying, shall go down
To the vile dust from whence he sprung,
Unwept, unhonour'd, and unsung.
(from "The Lay of the Last Minstrel")

This is how we have, in the past period tended to think about a person who was not loyal to something larger than himself. But there has been a long and irregular movement toward a wider object for our loyalty, not one that makes loyalty to the nation less, but makes loyalty to the whole species more. In the early 19th Century the French philosopher Montesquieu wrote:

> *If I knew something useful to my nation, but ruinous to another nation, I would not propose it to my ruler, because I am a man before I am a Frenchman, or rather because I am a man by necessity and a Frenchman only by chance of birth…. If I knew something useful to my country but prejudicial to Europe, or useful to Europe but prejudicial to the human race, I would consider it a crime to propose it.*

This expresses the direction we are trying to move. This is patriotism for the 21st Century.

Loyalty to one group has always meant that we had different standards for members of the in-group and those outside of it. We always have differentiated two different types of human beings and treated them very differently. In the very small world of the 21st

Century with the Internet, viruses and radioactive clouds which ignore national borders as if they were not there, we can no longer afford this luxury. There can only be one "Family of Man," one in-group—the entire human race. And this is where we are heading.

A number of years ago one of us (LLL) was talking to the social activist Abbie Hoffman of "The Chicago Seven" fame. He was, at that time, wanted by the FBI and had just returned from eight years "underground" which he had spent in plain sight organizing the successful defense of the ecology of the St. Lawrence River.

He said that he had recently been challenged at a meeting that he had only a negative program, not a positive one. "We know all the things that you are against," the speaker said. "What do you want?" What are you trying to accomplish?" Hoffman had replied, "What we want is a generation in which whenever a member of it walks down the street he will see three things that need to be corrected and set to work on one of them."

The philosopher and sociologist Karl Popper described two types of effort to change and improve society. One he calls "Utopian Engineering" and the other "Piecemeal Engineering." The utopian engineer designs a blueprint of what the ideal society should be and tries to set it up wholesale—to sweep away the old and start the new. Thus to start his Republic, Plato stated that all the inhabitants of a city over the age of ten should be forcibly exiled, leaving only those under that age and the educators who would become the philosopher kings. Then the Utopia could start and attain its goal in one giant step. Similarly Pol Pot in Cambodia who forcibly emptied all the cities in one week. Or the Stalinist Communists who deliberately starved to death the Kulaks (successful small farmers) in one Winter to make room for the new collectivization. Sending all the aristocrats to the guillotine in the French Revolution is another example.

The piecemeal engineer, on the other hand, is aware that perfection is, at the very least, far distant. The real task is to take one evil at a time—evil being regarded as that which is most destructive and painful to people—and to try to lessen it. Regarding as equal the claim of the people now living and those who will live in the future, the piecemeal engineer tries to reduce, one at a time, those factors which weigh most heavily on their lives and development. Since different engineers at any one time see different evils as the most pressing, there results a number of simultaneous pressures in the direction of making human life more free and having more possibilities of development and growth. But there is no attempt to sacrifice one group for the others. ("This generation is manure for the next," said the Utopian Engineer Bolsheviks of 1917 and the next following years.) Rather one works for specific causes to remove one thorn at a time from the human brow.

No one, of course, can make anybody else happy. Neither a person nor a group can do this. Both, however, can work to reduce the factors that make another person or group unhappy. Nor can you make another person develop or flower. You can work to reduce the factors which prevent the flowering.

The piecemeal engineer does not see any culture as a mere means of reaching toward another. He or she is not trying to reach an ideal state because there is no such thing. (In Gertrude Stein's words, "When you get there you find there is no there there.") The piecemeal kind of approach simply tries to remove one bar to human freedom and development at a time. The utopian idea that we can plan an ideal life for people in the future is an old, an attractive and a widespread one. Few of those who explored or advocated the matter have seen clearly the major problems inherent in it. (Karl Popper, Isaiah Berlin, Morris Raphael Cohen and Louis Mumford seem to me to have been the major exceptions.) The first problem is that it strongly tends to make its adherents ruthless and heedless of others in their drive to attain it. Idealistically they have envisioned the perfect way for the human race to live. Nothing must stand in its way. Literally it is such a wonderful omelet that it does not matter how many eggs get broken in the attempt to reach it. War, killing, persecution, torture are all justified by the great goal to be reached. This glorious end justifies all means. Thus, it leads to a belief that all other goals are errors or heresy since they are keeping the human race from fulfillment and therefore should be suppressed. If the goal is an infinite period (as it always is) of perfection then the tortures of the Spanish Inquisition were justified in inflicting a finite period of pain to reach it. Similarly there is justification for the SS anti-Semitic programs and the Stalinist Communist killing "deviationists" of all kinds.

Isaiah Berlin wrote in this context:

So long as only one ideal is the true goal, it will

*always seem to men that no means can be difficult,
no price too high, to do whatever is required to
reach the ultimate goal. Such certainty is one of
the great justifications of fanaticism, compulsion,
persecution.*

Karl Popper in his classic *The Open Society and
Its Enemies* has shown how any attempt to set up a
Utopia must misfire and lead to authoritarianism
and the destruction of dissenters ("Liquidation" was
the popular term for a long time), and the eventual
diversion of movement toward an entirely different goal
than was originally envisioned. This book, written far
before the end of the utopian engineering experiment
made in Russia in 1917, predicted in uncanny detail
the collapse of the USSR and what the outcome of such
an attempt must be.

Morris Raphael Cohen wrote of

*"...the fatal and desolating illusion that we can ever
have or bring about a heaven on Earth—an illusion
which has been the source of much that is noble but
also of that fierce fanaticism which has shut the
gates of mercy on mankind."*

Exactly what this ideal way of being would
actually be has never been widely agreed upon. We
have agreed that it would be the "end of history"
and, once achieved, we would dwell in an ideal state
forever. Nothing more would be needed and nothing
new would happen. These ideal states which various
groups of us have striven for in the belief that it was
the only right way for all, included a classless society,
that all humanity follow our particular interpretation

of the scripture we choose, Valhalla on Earth, that all sentient beings are freed from the wheel of things, that philosophers rule and all are in their proper places in a class society, that all humans live in harmony with our conception of nature, that we return to the Golden Age that existed before our own, any many others. However we envision a Utopia, it is so wonderful that any sacrifice of ourselves or others is well worth it. That the others may not agree is unfortunate, but they must be changed by any means for their own good.

The second basic problem with a Utopia is that if attained it would mean an end to growth, to change, to new ideas. Artists and thinkers would have to be very carefully watched and controlled—even Plato was aware of this—and it would mean chains about the human spirit for as long as it existed. This stultification, this insistence that we had reached the final goal and that there was no other place to go, that all dissent is error or treason is, once we look at it, obviously a horror and, literally, a dead end for humanity. We can not go really forward by assuming that we know everything that will be known in the future and can plan the lives people in the future will want to live. Trying this route does not free our children's children, it imprisons them.

A patriotism for the 21st Century is a loyalty to the entire human race and to their right to solve the problems they have in their own way. It is a commitment to their freedom to design their own lives.

The one thing of which we can be sure is that in the future they will have problems of which we do not even dream. No Classical Greek or Roman, no Medieval person, could conceive of problems like destruction of the world ecology, overpopulation, giant business monopolies or atomic bombs.

It is impossible to predict what problems will arise in the future, what species life or species death conundrums we will face as we move forward in technology and outward in space. It is, therefore, equally impossible to predict what personality types we will need, what kinds of individuals will be most adept when needed, most likely to be able to solve them. It is therefore part of our loyalty to the future to offer as wide a latitude as possible to different personality types, to different developments of personality. This is true of both individuals and cultures, of persons and societies and organizations. Short of danger to ourselves and our children, we want and need as wide a variety of human personalities available as possible. "Mankind," wrote J.S. Mill, "are greater gainers by suffering each other to live as seems good to themselves than by compelling each to live as seem good to the rest." Elsewhere Mill wrote, "…the only unfailing and permanent source of improvement is liberty, since by it there are as many possible sources of improvement as there are individuals."

This is certainly not a new idea. Alexander von Humboldt in 1792 and Alexis de Tocqueville in 1850, for example, pointed out that two things are necessary for human development and for growth in new directions and flexibility in the face of adversity. These two are freedom and a variety of personality structures, customs, beliefs, orientations. Today we would also use other descriptive phrases such as "ways of being in the world."

Censoring ideas or art stultifies thought and growth. It makes for an orthodoxy that reduces individuality and thereby makes less our resources for solving new and unprecedented problems. A concept is a tool and we can not know what tools will be needed in the future. Further, without available criticism of ideas they lose their strength and validity. They become schools instead of tools with sharp cutting edges. In Mill's words, "He who knows only his own side of the case knows little of that." Later he writes, "Both teachers and learners go to sleep at their post as soon as there is no enemy in sight."

In particular it is important to keep an atmosphere of freedom for art. The artists help us to see in new ways, to question our accepted views. They are not only the spearheads of new developments, they also sound the warning when our old views are paralyzing us. Like the canaries that miners used to take down into the mines to warn them of gas before they themselves could sense it, the artist sounds a signal when our customs and ways of viewing reality are preventing any movement. In the words of the artist Paul Klee, "The artist does not reproduce the visible; rather he makes things visible." We humans tend to be much more one-sided than many-sided. To remain viable in the unpredictable future we need many different kinds of individuals and different kinds of alive ideas.

Art being free is everyone's concern. All that is needed is an absence of censorship. (This, however, does not imply government support for art. If there is this, it always ultimately implies an "academy" point of view. Government support inevitably means government control.) It is everyone's business to see that art is not censored but it is not everyone's business to support it. It is no one else's business how the artist makes his or her living, just that they are not prevented. In the art field the opposite of Gresham's Law operates—eventually good art drives out bad art. A Van Gogh or a Mozart may starve to death in the meantime, but it is their business how they spend their lives. It is, of course, a very different matter if local communities wish to support a repertory theatre, an exhibit hall, or a symphony orchestra. In these cases, if the artist's works are not accepted, he or she can go elsewhere.

CHAPTER 5

A FOURTH OF JULY SPEECH FOR THE TWENTY-FIRST CENTURY

IT IS OUR TRADITION in the United States for politicians and statesmen to make speeches on our Independence Day, the Fourth of July. In these they extol our country and define our patriotism. The Independence Day speech presented here has not yet been given. Hopefully a version of it will be in the near future. Imagine what a difference it will make to us and the whole world when we have a President who will say something like this.

"My fellow citizens of the wonderful country we all love, this is a time to recall and celebrate the ideals of our country and the men and women who have lived by them and sometimes died for them. We sing the praises of the great Americans who established our democracy—George Washington, Thomas Jefferson, Crispus Attucks, Haym Solomon, John Adams and Paul Revere. And those who fought to keep the freedoms they won—Abraham Lincoln, Emma Goldman, Andrew Goodman, Martin Luther King, Jr., Ike Eisenhower, John F. Kennedy. And the thousands of others we can not name here,

one of whom rests symbolically in our Tomb of the Unknown Soldier. And the others who fought for freedom in battle or in our halls of government. It is due to these that we stand here, alive and free in the most wonderful country in history.

"And we remember also the words that epitomize their struggles—"Life, Liberty and the Pursuit of Happiness," "Liberty for All," "Equal Justice Under Law," The Four Freedoms."

"We can be proud of what we have done and where we are. But where do we go from here? There is so much more to do to fulfil and celebrate our nation. We must make sure that every citizen is free from want and fear and is so secure that it is possible for him or her to engage in "The Pursuit of Happiness."

"Daniel Webster declared "Freedom and Union. One and Inseparable. Now and Forever." And it is true that unless we are all together in the achievement of our hard won rights, no one is secure in them.

"Our future as a nation lies in what we do and in our children. And they are one and the same.

"Is there a five-year-old child in Appalachia or in an inner-city ghetto or on an Indian Reservation that is hungry and cold? Then no child in America, not yours or mine, is safe from hunger and cold. It is your child shivering and hungry because it is a human child. The ones you are raising in your homes are yours, but so is this one. If you turn away from him, you turn away from yours. And if you turn away from him, what are you teaching him and your own children? What sort of lesson for the future are you an example of? What are you teaching them about America?

"And do yours now know that you care enough about them that you are concerned that when they grow up they will have the opportunity and the freedom to work toward the kind of life that they will most enjoy and that will most fulfil them?

And that while they are working at this they will have clean air and water and a functioning planet? That you are concerned enough about the future to vote only for people who will help sustain their home—this lovely planet? That when you buy your car you will be concerned as much about your children's future as you are about the opinions of your neighbors and buy the car with the lowest poison emission rate?

"*I have spoken of the child in Appalachia or in an inner-city ghetto or on a Reservation in our West. These are our children starving and cold and this is a sign that we have barely begun our journey. When every child there is warm and fed and loved and feels safe we will have made the first step on the journey of which our forefathers dreamed.*

"*But the second step follows and the first can never be really completed without it. Let me tell you about a lovely nine-year-old girl named Ama. She has big brown eyes and is very thin. She lives in a village in Africa. Her parents have died of AIDS, as have half the adults in her village. She has not eaten anything for two days and little before that. There is no one to hold or comfort her and she is crying herself to sleep tonight, curled up into a ball and holding her stomach because it hurts so much. She is very frightened. She will starve to death soon unless one of the truckers on the road that passes the village sees her and decides that she would make a good prostitute and rapes her and then puts her to work. If that happens she will certainly die of AIDS by the age of nineteen or twenty.*

"*Now* **THIS IS WRONG!** *We all know it and feel it. It is wrong that tonight Ama should be crying in her hut alone and unable to sleep because she is so hungry and lonely and terrified. We may be sorry about all the starving children in the world but, if we let ourselves picture Ama, this nine-year-old girl with big brown eyes, all alone and unfed, we feel compassion and indignation that this should be allowed to happen. And when* *we are no longer afraid to feel our compassion and indignation we can begin to act. We can not look at her and say to her, "You live too far away and there are too many like you. There is nothing for you here, Ama."*

"All children are our children. If the Starry Flag does not mean this, it does not mean anything else it says when it waves above us.

"We, you and I, can not save all the Amas. There are too many. But we can help. And all of us will sleep better if we do.

"We can each adopt one child through the organizations set up for this, for a very little each month you can give this child the food, shelter, medicines and schooling it needs. You can exchange pictures and letters to the child and show that your patriotism to the United States is not less, but your patriotism to the whole human race is more.

"You can help support organizations like UNICEF and Medicines Sans Frontieres which reach out to comfort children like Ama.

"You can make sure that your children and Ama will have a green and beautiful world to live in by being concerned about the ecology, by buying cars that endanger the environment the least and goods that are biodegradable and do not last and last until our planet is an unlivable garbage dump. You can recycle. Once you let yourself care many more ways will occur to you.

"And you can vote for people who will be concerned about these things and about Ama, and only for these people regardless of what political party they belong to.

"What does it mean to be an American? Here on the Fourth of July in the first part of the 21st Century we look forward and back and say.

"To be an American means to be fortunate indeed. It is to live in a country where we believe in freedom and in justice under law for all. It means working for these things for all of

us. And "Us" in our ever smaller and still lovely planet no longer means only the United States. Today US means all of the human race. As we grew from members of a state—South Carolina, Massachusetts, Virginia—now we begin to move toward being also members of a greater nation—that includes all human beings.

"We live in a great union of states which will someday be a part of a great union of nations. Until that time we are all citizens of Earth. Let us protect that citizenship and our world home with our legacy from the past and our hopes for the future.

"The United States is a glorious place to live and it is an honor to be a citizen. But we do not stand alone. Our borders touch oceans and lands that touch other oceans and lands and there is no stopping place all around the globe. We breathe air that flows over all the continents and back again. A forest purifies it for all of us. A careless factory contaminates it for all of us. We are human and each of us has a loyalty, a patriotism not only to one family, one community, one great nation, but also to the whole race of which we are each a part."

───────────────────────

Think what it would mean for the future if the head of your government was the kind of person who would make a Fourth of July speech like that. Perhaps the next time you are in a voting booth you might ask yourself if whomever you are supporting is, or could grow into, such a person. If not, take a look at the others running for office.

CHAPTER 6

THE LIMITATIONS OF INDIVIDUAL FREEDOM

WE CAN NOT MICROMANAGE the future or even decide what political or social shape it will have. We can work to improve the lot and condition of the members of our species. We can work to protect all children, to encourage diversity, to remove injustices, to take out one thorn from the brow of humanity at a time. We can protect our fragile planet and clean up the poisons leached into it by our past.

Beyond this it is futile to try to go. Tomorrow's decisions will be based on what people know and believe tomorrow and we can not know what that will be except that it will be different than what we know and believe today.

It may well be that the future will decide that the best political structure for them is built on the village or independent cities or a nation or a whole federation or an Empire or something else within our present comprehension or outside of it. We can not know, but we do know that, whatever it is, we want the children and the old and the weak to be protected. We can get to work protecting these and know that we are moving in the right direction.

Different kinds of problems need different kinds of people and different kinds of abilities to solve them. We can work to permit and encourage as wide a diversity of lifestyles and world views as possible and know that we, in doing this, are working to ensure that there will be the resources available to solve the as yet unknown and inconceivable problems of the future.

We live as though we stand knocking on doors which are still closed to us. The present is suspended between a no-longer and a not-yet and we can not tell the shape of the not-yet. This has always been true and will be true in the future. It was true in classical Greek and Roman times and in the Medieval period. No one can say what lies ahead for the human race. We can only act so as to make it more likely that there is a future for us and that it is a better time for human beings to live in than the present or the past. We do this most effectively in little ways, removing one inequity at a time and expanding our freedoms one and then another one.

I have written here of the need, in the new patriotism, to work toward new and greater diversities and more and more freedom for the individual. Only in this way can we hope to ensure that our children's children can continue to solve their problems. But what are the limits? Where do we stop?

In one part of Arthur Koestler's book *Thieves in the Night*, set in 1937 then Palestine, a small group of Jewish settlers are surrounded by a larger and better armed Arab force. The Arabs are intent on killing `the Jews, most of whom have fled from German death camps. During a temporary halt in the firing one politically very liberal Jew asks another if he does not see the Arab point of view. The other replies, "We can not afford to see their point of view."

And there are times when we can not afford to give the opposite point of view as much validity as our own. If someone is intent on killing you and your children and is coming at you with a knife and will not listen to anything you say, this is simply not the time to be concerned with the center of gravity of their world-view, what is most real to them, the injustices they suffered in childhood, or their ambitions for their children. It is simply time to prevent him from killing you and hopefully doing this in a painful enough way that he will not be tempted to repeat the process at some later date.

The critical question for our ethical mandate is: *Under what conditions do you ignore the other person's point of view, do you limit their freedom and their expression of their diversity?* Justice Oliver Wendell Holmes provided part of the answer in his famous statement on constitutionally guaranteed liberties. He said, "Your right to wave your fist ends one inch from my nose."

This provides the basis for the answer to our critical question. The answer is that any individual or group has the right to follow its own directives or whims, to succeed in its endeavors or to go to its own heaven or hell in its own ways until its behavior comes threatening within one inch of our own nose, one foot of our children's nose, one yard of the nose of the human race.

If we had read *Mein Kampf* before Hitler started his armies moving, we would have seen from his clear statements that he was within the limits of one inch from our nose and one foot from our children's nose. We would then have realized that we could not afford to be concerned with his point of view and stopped him quickly and easily at the Rhineland. The Iraqi attempted development of atomic weaponry, with their history of aggression whenever they thought they could get away with it, was a clear violation of the one inch, one foot and one yard rule. (Any atomic war is a clear threat to the life of our species. With the present proliferation of atomic weapons, one exploded bomb will lead to who knows where.) One thing we know about war is that it leads to the unpredictable. And there are today certain surprises we can not afford to risk. At a certain point of a disagreement if the Rule of Three is invaded, the threatened individual must become "unreasonable" in the sense that the jurist Edmund Cahn used the term. Negotiation ends, a flat viewpoint is taken and a course of action must be followed. There is no further room for negotiation. When warnings and protests to the world's governments failed, the Israelis correctly took action and destroyed Iraq's nuclear capability in a surprise bombing raid. (No one thanked them but we all breathed easier.)

Each individual may only be controlled by society in order to stop him from doing harm to others. There are many difficult border areas here ranging from abortion to drugs to the compulsory wearing of seat belts and crash helmets. In each of these the basic question is: "Is the behavior private or does it threaten others?" Some of these problems will need careful study of the individual cases. Others can be solved by direct application of the rule. Thus consensual sex between adults is clearly their own business, but child abuse and education of children is everybody's business. All children are our children. (The actress, Mrs. Patrick Campbell, said she did not care what people did sexually "as long as they don't do it in the street and frighten the horses!")

————————————

This concept has implications for many types of moral problems. Let us suppose that we learn that a helpless old person is secretly being kept prisoner and abused next door. Where does this guideline lead us? On first glance it appears that no part of the rule of three is invoked. We must simply let it go on as a private matter.

Looking more deeply, however, we see that we must take action under the one-inch rule. Each of us may be weak and helpless one day. In order to protect ourselves in this eventuality, in order to ensure that *we* will be protected at that time, we must make sure that we live in a social climate where the old, the weak, and the helpless *are* protected and not exploited. This is like taking out accident insurance.

Unless there are basic rules to protect the weak and helpless humans, we are left open to the cold winds. We *will* if we live long enough be weak and helpless compared to someone else. The one-foot rule makes it imperative that we protect ourselves then by setting up the rules (take out the annuities—insurance policies) now.

We do not live only in a biological but also in

a social ecology. Both must be geared to nurture and protect us during the various stages of our life. Retirement insurance is one way. Equally necessary is the insurance of living in a society that by its rules provides social insurance. Public duties are an integral part of private self-protection.

If people believe that they can kill or exploit someone else for private gain or whim and not under the law, where does this leave us in the future? No matter how strong we are now, the future is uncertain and the ideas may be turned against us later and we are unprotected. The philosopher Mary Midgley put it, "As the MacBeths found, such ideas can not be kept in isolated compartments, they often spill over…"

The situation is similar to that of boat and ship sailors. Unless we are watchful and responsive when others needs help, we can not expect it when we do. Unless the social system is such that you and everyone else is aware of, stops and helps those on a sinking ship, we will not be helped when our own ship is foundering. For our own protection we need a system that will protect those who have lost control of their own destiny whether this loss is due to storm winds and high waves, age, incapacity, or more powerful and ruthless others.

A second aspect of this would be in the one-yard rule. We can not expect there to be a protective attitude toward the human race if we see around us the weak and helpless members of the race being exploited. This gives a clear double message. If we wish the race to be protected, we must protect its members.

We can not go back to the classical Greek system of regarding as really human only adult, affluent, male citizens. Or the Enlightenment view of only males. (The excellent educational system of Rousseau was only for boys.) Nor can we return to the Early American view of only male Caucasians. Nor to V.I. Lenin's "What is moral is what is advantageous to the proletarian class." Clearly all human beings is the smallest group we can be concerned about. The one-yard rule is the most complex of all. Either it is the whole human race or it does not cohere. The term and idea of "The Family of Man" is a truism and a dream. It is a necessary goal if we wish to survive. We will be a family of man or our left-behind artifacts will be examined by the species that follows us as we examine the petrified footprints, bones and eggs of the dinosaurs.

The American Indian Iroquois Six-Nation Confederacy was a democratic society which, for example, gave women an equal vote and political voice at a time when this was unknown in Europe, the Middle East or Asia. It had as its great law the *Haudenosaunee*. "In all our deliberations we must be mindful of the impact of our decisions on the seven generations to follow us."

We must, today, take this one step further if we wish to survive our knowledge of atomics and our growing knowledge of space travel. We must begin to say, "In all our deliberations we must be mindful of the impact of our decisions on the future survival of the human race."

If an old person is being abused and exploited behind locked doors, the social system that is necessary to protect me in the future has broken down. I repair it or face the possible consequences.

In addition, if Group A militarily invades and

takes over Group B a social climate is produced in which we may be next. To protect ourselves and our children, we need to ensure that this is not done. We can not say that Group A is simply following its own morés and should be left alone. We need insurance for our children that they will live in a climate that protects them from military invasion. Being in a strong military position oneself is not very much protection compared to a social climate. The French in 1938 believed themselves to have the strongest army in the world and to be secure behind the mightiest fortification line ever built. They, with the rest of the world, permitted the destruction of Ethiopia, Austria, Spain, Czechoslovakia, and a general climate of lawlessness. A few weeks in 1939 showed how weak a reed were their army and fortifications.

On the other hand, if Group A and Group B decide that they wish to batter each other and are stupid enough to settle disagreements with force, that is their affair unless atomic fallout is going to land on us or our children. Then, in Mill's words, "...the case is taken out of the province of liberty and placed in that of morality or law."

A deer is attacked by wolves. Under the rule of three and its implications I have no responsibility. I will never be a deer and neither will my children. There is no threat here to me, to human children, or to the human race. Unless I am competing with the wolves for food, there is no reason for me to act.

And when I do, it tends to backfire. We killed off the cougar who were preying on "the beautiful deer" in the Grand Canyon area of the Western United States. The deer multiplied since we disturbed the balance of nature, ate up all the local vegetation, changed the ecology of the area and destroyed much of its life and deer sustaining ability. In the barren landscape that resulted they largely succumbed to illness and starvation.

Thus from the viewpoint of this ethical guideline we actively interfere to protect the helpless person, who we ourselves may become in time, who is being abused next door. Further, child abuse and child prostitution and forced suttee (burning a widow on the pyre of her husband) are public problems. Non-forced suttee with other viable options is a private matter. Abortion is a private matter. Selling drugs to children is of public concern. The education and development of children are public matters.

Although many cases must be decided on an individual case-by-case basis, the interpretation is often fairly obvious. Being drunk is a private affair. For a soldier, a physician or a policeman to be drunk on duty is a public affair. Driving a car on public streets while drunk is a public matter. Suicide—except that of children, is a private matter.

In this view, as in that of John Stewart Mill, each adult may only be controlled by society in order to stop his from doing harm to others. "in the part [of his conduct] which merely concerns himself, his rule is, of right, absolute. Over himself, over his own body and mind, the individual is sovereign."

The One Yard Rule has other implications. We face unknown problems of human survival in the future. What these will be we can not now even guess except that they will be new and difficult. We may or may not be able to solve them, but to give us the best possible chance to do so we will need available all our resources in ability to think and to act. Any general procedure that reduces the amount of available intellectual or other ability lessens the probability of our being able to solve these problems and therefore to survive as a species. These procedures which reduce the probability of our surviving include social customs which prevent certain parts of the population from functioning at its highest level, its highest potential. Systematic discrimination against any large group, or gender, prevents them from moving toward their potential and thereby reduces the overall ability of the human race to solve the new and as-yet-unimagined problems is lessened.

Therefore systematic discrimination against any sizeable group of humans violates the one-yard rule and is everybody's problem.

It is impossible to predict what problems will arise in the future, what species life or species death conundrums we will face as we move forward in technology and outward in space. It is, therefore, equally impossible to predict what personality types we will need, what kinds of individual will be most adept when needed, most likely to be able to solve them. It is therefore part of our need to survive as a race to offer as wide a latitude as possible to different personality types, to different developments of personality. This is true of both individuals and cultures, of persons and societies and organizations. This, of course, is limited to those who do not run afoul of the one inch, one foot, one yard rule. Short of danger to ourselves and our children, we want and need as wide a variety of human personalities available as possible. "Mankind," wrote J.S. Mill, "are greater gainers by suffering each other to live as seems good to themselves than by compelling each to live as seem good the rest. …the only unfailing and permanent source of improvement is liberty, since by it there are as many possible sources of improvement as there are individuals."

CHAPTER 7

CHANGING OUR SCHOOLS
TO CHANGE THE FUTURE

IT HAS LONG BEEN a truism that a school system turns out graduates who fit into and can function in the society that organized it and pays for it. For our society the "three Rs" are essential. In order to survive in it a person *must* be able to read, write and do basic arithmetic. Ingenuity and love in teaching them is essential for a good teacher even if they are not found too often in the schoolrooms.

The schools *must* teach the three Rs. Today, however, we know enough to be able not only to teach our students what they need to survive in our culture, but also how to orient them to improving it and to helping it move in the direction of the society for which we hope.

The first step in raising and educating children who can have their basic loyalty to the human race as a whole and to a safe environment for their children and grandchildren is for us to recognize as critical that children need to feel safe. Unless they do feel this way, all our other efforts to move into a fuller future are likely to fail. So long as we continue to betray this need, children will grow up to be damaged adults who can not fully care for themselves, others, or the human race.

Children *must* have two things in order to feel safe. First, they must know that adults care enough for them to be actively working for their safety. The goal of safety need not (and can not) ever be fully attained, so long as children know that we adults are **actively trying** to protect them. This means in the home, in the school, in the immediate environment, and in the world at large.

The second thing that children need is the knowledge that their own efforts can have effects— that they have the potential to act in ways that will be helpful. This can only come from experience in working at those tasks appropriate to their age. They learn in this way that they are not helpless and weak, but that they have "environmental competence," that their actions can have a positive effect on their world.

This is the beginning, and the necessary beginning, of the change to a new patriotism. What I have been saying here about the basic need of children is not farfetched theorizing. We now know enough about children and how they become adults to state unequivocally that these facts are true.

The second step in putting into place any real program for our children is to realize that one of the central problems is that we usually believe that there is somewhere a method of changing the values of young people in a positive way without changing ourselves.

This is a fatal fallacy.

If we are searching for a theory and a curriculum that will improve the development and behavior of students, but not our own, we are on a hopeless quest. Many school administrators and politicians want this. They say, in effect, to the educators, "Teach us how to educate the students in our schools to a better moral development without changing ourselves, the general structure of the schools, the relationships within it, how we ourselves behave, and so forth." This can not be done.

The educator Lawrence Kohlberg responded to one such request, this one by a school principal, as follows:

> *Helping you would mean dealing with real life dilemmas, that is school dilemmas. And dealing with behavior means not only what is just and fair in school dilemmas, but encouraging action to make the school more just. That means trying to promote fairness in teachers' behavior as well as in student behavior. So, if you'd like, I'd consider counseling with you and the teachers to make the school a more just community.[1]*

The classic studies of Hartshorne and May (1928-1932) and many others since then have shown that didactic instruction, lecturing about honesty and morality, "character education" classes, had almost no lasting or significant effect on either students' moral judgment or on their moral behavior.

Teaching loyalty and ethics in the abstract is a dubious procedure at best. We learn an ethical system by acting accordingly to its precepts. Here we learn by doing. The famous story of the philosopher who wanted to learn to swim before he ventured into the water is relevant in this context.[2]

Between the ages of eight and eleven children begin to be actively concerned with larger questions than those which were central earlier. When 5,000 elementary school children were asked what questions they would like to have answered their responses included the great moral questions, the ethical problems that philosophers have been asking since far before our records go back. And we answer these questions for them by our actions, not our words. Children follow their adult guides as they actually live, not as they preach.[3]

The educator Philip Jackson invented the term "hidden curriculum" to refer to ninety percent of what goes on in a classroom. As long as the hidden curriculum, what one is really taught in a school, includes how to be treated and to act as one of a crowd, how to accept the absolute authority of an appointed stranger, how to work at and learn what one is ordered to from above, how to live and survive in an environment which is concerned with what you do to a school subject and not what the subject does to you, that democratic behavior and individual difference are to be discussed, not lived, that originality and creativity tend to get you into trouble—so long as lessons such as these are the main things taught in our schools—we will not have much improvement in our ability to move forward to a new and larger loyalty.[4]

One day, while working on this book, the phone

rang. Would I (LLL) serve on a committee trying to develop methods of teaching ethical behavior to children? My first reaction was, "How do we teach ethics to grownups first?"

But after my initial negative response I knew that, ethically speaking, I had to try to think about teaching ethics, teaching the meaning of patriotism to children. And I realized that over the past years of thinking about this issue I had come up with some answers that might be useful.

When our daughter was about eight years old and she saw the Biafran children starving to death on the television screen, she became anxious and fearful. We tried to reassure her, but nothing made any difference until we suggested that she help us raise money, collect canned food and blankets, and join us on a candlelight parade at the UN. She stopped feeling scared and we observed a new light of pride in her.

A social worker in a small town in upstate New York told us that her community was a war zone, overcome by drugs, crime, angry young people, decaying schools. At the opening assembly on the first day of school a new high school principal (much against his Board's wishes) told the children there would be no classes the first week of school until the community was cleaned up—that no one could concentrate on learning when it looked as if a bomb had fallen on the town. At first the impoverished, deprived kids in high school laughed in glee. This was "Cool!" a time for some more wild and dangerous games. Not so. The classes had to sign in each morning and, with one or more teachers, were given assignments such as cleaning the courtyard in front of three buildings, raking, digging and planting pumpkins and other late Fall vegetables in a vacant lot, the food to be donated to a "Meals on Wheels" program. They had to pull all the tires and garbage out of the lake in the park, volunteer six hours a day as helpers in a public day care center, a senior citizens' center or a hospital, under the supervision of the professional staff in each place. A special role for seniors was to answer calls from people asking for specific referral to clinics related to child abuse, drug addiction, suicide threats.

Most of the people in the community were outraged. How could these kids be responsible? How could they take on jobs for which people need careful training, new skills? A week later, back at the assembly, there were committees of teachers and children to report. With very few exceptions, everyone had worked hard and done well. The student body voted to continue this work after school, each student, one day a week, for which they would get special credit in social studies.

Wherever and whenever young people have been challenged to be a part of the answer, to join with adults, the results have been spectacular. What this means is that teaching patriotism or ethics at home or in a classroom has become almost meaningless as our children look at the world today. The answer we can give them is that we understand how hopeless they must feel. We know they feel adults don't truly care about them.

This is a succinct way of making it perfectly clear that children need action and role models, not baseball players who gamble and take drugs, not people who steal, in banks or on the street—not politicians who lie. They need us, their parents and teachers, relatives, friends and neighbors, who do care but often feel too despairing to take action. *Taking action can save us as well as our children.* The only answer to serious social problems is to do something about them. Of course we have no guarantee it will work, but a basic ethical principle is that you have to keep trying even if you have little hope of winning. When we show concern for our total environment, when we express our loyalty to the entire human race, decency and kindness to each other follows.

This idea is not new, nor is it restricted to the adolescent and above years. Since the 1940s the City and Country School in New York City has had a "job program." At third grade level, at eight, for example, the children run the school post office which includes a serious job of maintaining all the communications within the school. Out of that they study communication and quite a number of related fields. The social studies arises in part from the tasks that the children actually do in and for their school.

Children in nursery school and kindergarten can bake healthy bran muffins for children who are homeless and living in shelters. Children in the grade school years can give up seeing some of the garbage movies they beg for, and use the money for AIDS research. High school kids can give direct service to others, such as helping to serve meals to unemployed workers in a church. Schools can invite elderly people in a nursing home to come see a play and bring their theatre productions to a round of nursing homes and senior centers. Children can develop work teams to help clean up the papers thrown on the ground in a park. Local service agencies nearly all need volunteers.

Older children can assist in younger classes. What has happened when such programs are developed is that all the children do far better in their schoolwork in a climate of mutual caring and cooperation. And they learn with and from us about being part of a community and being part of the human race.

In a growing number of public high schools students participate in a project of Amnesty International. They join in one of 3,000 "adoption groups," each of which adopt one of more prisoners who are held unjustly. They write letters to presidents, prison officials, legislators, etc., on behalf of the unjustly imprisoned.

In Bergenfield, New Jersey high school juniors and seniors staff an aid-to-senior-citizens project. Between 7:30 and 9:30 each morning they telephone elderly people who live alone to see if they are all right. In one year this resulted in thirty-seven emergency visits to senior citizens by paramedics when there was an emergency that prevented the phone from being answered.[5]

At St. Xavier College in Cincinnati scholarships are given to two groups—to athletes and to community volunteers who are prepared to work ten hours a week in social agencies, hospitals, etc. Athletes are required to pass all subjects as well. New York University students go to a public park in groups of four or more with a police officer. Their purpose is to make the park safe for everyone. They must also attend weekly meetings and write a term paper for which they receive regular course credit.

According to the National Students Volunteer Program (NSVP) headquarters in Washington, large and constantly increasing numbers of students on

American campuses are now regularly involved in some form of voluntary social action. The range is very great. It involves programs from free breakfasts for slum children to meals delivered to the elderly, from drug and emergency hotlines to eco-watch organizations, from teaching literacy to ex-convicts to counseling at abortion clinics, from voter registration to law-for-laymen, and to many others. This is indeed "piecemeal engineering" in the best sense of the word. They range widely from promoting social change to short term and immediate relief, from hands-on programs to theoretical study of community needs.[6]

Experiments on this approach are going on, little by little, all over the Western world, on all levels of education.

At the University of Hacettepe, on the outskirts of Ankara, students registering for the medical school are assigned responsibility for the health of a Turkish family living in a slum area of the city. Throughout their years of study they act as "medical friend" of the family—and in this they have, naturally, the backing of the faculty. When they ultimately receive the degree, much of their knowledge of community medicine has not been learnt from books or lectures; it has been acquired at first hand. Moreover, the development of a sense of social responsibility towards the sick has not been left to chance; it has been built into their course of study from the very first day.[7]

A program showing both moral education and incidental learning is described by Sinclair Goodlad in his excellent overview of student social action programs, their problems and advantages, in England.

As a result of an initiative of this kind, a group of Imperial College engineering undergraduates studied methods of delivering hot food to old people in Hackney (England) during the academic year 1972-3. In 1972-3 the borough of Hackney supplied over 380,000 hot meals to old people who were either housebound or who could walk to their nearest club for a subsidised meal. Some of the food had to meet special dietary requirements, for medical or religious reasons; some was specially prepared for physically or mentally handicapped people. On an average day in Hackney, some 1,500 meals are distributed. The deliveries, which start at 11:30 a.m., have to reach any dwelling in the borough. Great attention is given to ensuring that the meals arrive regularly, for regular visits can be the focal point in the daily routine of old people who are socially isolated…

The students' project was to examine the system for delivering hot food and see if it could be improved. Some of the problems were: how to keep food hot when a helper climbs four floors; to deliver food in a block of flats with no lift; how to package food so that the package can be easily delivered, but has a lid which does not cut the hands of the kitchen staff (which aluminum foil tends to do) and is easily opened by a ninety-year-old woman with arthritis; how to design hot-boxes with optimum power supply, temperature control, insulation, weight, accessibility, etc.; how to achieve the optimal routing of vehicles—taking account of parking restrictions, engine performance characteristics, difficulty of access to each dwelling on a route, etc….

Six students were given a complete free hand to examine the existing system and report on it, with suggestions for improvements. They considered radical solutions—such as that the best way to provide hot food for old people would be for their neighbors to cook it or that—if the visits of the helpers were more valued than the food—it might be better to distribute and heat the food separately (supplying small ovens to the old people and distributing blast-frozen food in an unhurried routine which would facilitate greater social contact). However, a conventional meals-on-wheels system is littered with interesting technical problems through the solution of which students can acquire considerable technical knowledge. For example, students were able to study the routing of vehicles with a computer—learning a new computer language in order to do so.[8]

The need for moral education has been long known and clearly recognized. In 1918, The National Education Association of the United States appointed a special commission to prepare a statement of goals called "Purposes of the School." The completed document had as its first and foremost goal, "Provide the child with a sense of ethical behavior in human relationships."

Although the need for moral education has been widely known (even though the way to implement this has not been clearly understood), fashions do change in education as the climate of a society changes. The 1918 document was superseded by The National Education Association in 1960. The new commission (headed by the President of Columbia Teachers College) got right to the point. It started:

The central purpose of the school is to develop the rational powers of man. The basic subjects for thinking and reasoning: English, Mathematics, Science and History.[9]

FASHIONS CHANGE, BUT THE old view of education, that its purpose is "to make the pupils smart and make them good" has generally underlain educational policy. In the new age in which we are living since Hiroshima, there is a necessary new goal—to develop human beings who can survive and help the race survive in the atomic and space age. Here, as never before, the words of Theodore Roosevelt ring ominously, "To educate a person in mind and not in morals is to educate a menace to society." Or, in more recent parlance, every student who goes through our educational system emerges as either a part of the problem or a part of the solution.[10]

Robert Starrett has distinguished between acts of mercy and acts of justice. In his terms, bringing food to the poor at Christmas is an act of mercy, working to change the social conditions which trap people into poverty is an act of justice. Children may start with acts of mercy, but must be helped by the educational system to go on to acts of justice.[11]

The educator Dorothy Cohn has described our present understanding of the development of morality and patriotism in the child by showing how it begins with the parents' admonitions and examples, and the desire both for parental love and to escape punishment. As the child grows these are modified by the need to belong to peer groups and to work out the problems of belonging, friendship, and so forth. It is in this actual experience and work that ethical values become a part of the soon-to-be adult. What started as a relationship with adults is solidified, changed and developed by group activities.

When these include groups with larger goals than

their own individual needs, both the person (the individual child) and the social group are helped to develop in healthy and constructive ways. This is what Friedrich Froebel meant by *Gleidganzes*—a whole that develops because it is, in turn, part of a larger whole.

And one may make no mistake about this. By our examples and admonitions, by focusing or not focusing our children's group activities, we do teach patriotism and a moral code. The only choice we have is what moral code we teach and what and how large a grow we teach our children to be loyal to.

Certainly it is true, as many writers have pointed out, that the schools must also teach moral behavior by example—the teacher by caring about these values, the school by acting as if they were important. Thomas Linkona, in his important *Educating for Character*, gives many examples of how this can be done. However, it is necessary to go beyond this. "To develop responsibility, young people need to have responsibility. To learn to care, they must perform caring actions."[12] Many public high schools are now beginning to mandate some form of public service as a graduation requirement. In the face of the increasing demoralization of the ethical climate in the early 21st Century this is progressing faster than is generally realized. The high school systems of Atlanta, Detroit and St. Louis, all sizeable cities, now have this requirement with a minimum seventy-five hours of service. An increasing number of schools are affiliating with the Giraffe Project which gives awards to people who "stick their necks out" by taking unusual action for ethical reasons. Cross-age tutoring and Big Brother and Big Sister projects are being developed in ever larger numbers of schools.

A list of these and similar programs is given by Fred Newman and Robert Rutter in their *A Profile of High School Community Programs*.[13] As there has been a growing recognition by educators that simply knowing right from wrong or having taken verbal courses in ethics is essential, but far from enough, more and more action programs are being instituted. One educator wrote, "We overwhelm children with all the suffering and evil in the world, but do we enable them to act?" More and more this question is being addressed with programs that give children a sense of what Newman has called "environmental competence," the knowledge that they can make a difference, make a real impact on others and on the society in which they live.[14] This can only come about through experiences in which they *do* make a difference. Newman has made it clear that if children do not learn to act and take action for the sake of justice and compassion, their verbal learning in this area will have little effect on them or on others. Developing a sense of environmental competence must become a major part and goal of our educational system.

A good deal of recent research has shown that one major reason that so little is being done to prevent nuclear war and to protect our failing environment is the belief that individual action can make no real difference—that individuals have no "environmental competence."[15]

And surely children can join us in supporting those organizations that are fighting the good fight against drugs and crime and terrible prison conditions and the proliferation of guns in every classroom and the poisoning of the planet. One seventh grade teacher told me, "I teach science by studying what pesticides do to crops. I teach math by fundraising projects for Greenpeace. I teach the sacredness of human life by assignment homework which is to watch different TV programs and count the number of killings, the number of minutes devoted to violence. We write letters to the advertising agencies that sponsor death and destruction. What else is a classroom for?"

I'm sure she spends time on the spelling in those letters, and sees that children add, subtract, multiply and divide when they figure what it costs to run a Greenpeace or Forever Wild sale, and what the margin of profit will be. When our homes and our classrooms are clearly in the service of improving human life on this earth, our children will become less angry, there will be less feeling of rejection, and in that climate learning can take place.

Of course we need to point to all the good people who care and live righteous lives, but the message will be lost until we say to our children, "Help us to change the world." Ethics begins with that message.[16]

This, of course, is far from the full answer needed to change the ethical climate in the world in the early 21st Century. As this entire book has tried to illustrate, we need much more. It is, however, a step we can take and is the kind of step that has proven itself of real value and is practical. It is "piecemeal engineering" rather than "Utopian engineering." It is the kind of approach that sets an example and a model for our children. The old Chinese proverb asks how one sets out on the longest journey in the world. The answer is "By putting out the left foot."

In no way does this approach rule out such methods

of teaching ethnical behavior as the cognitive-development methodology developed by Lawrence Kohlberg. These can only be an aid as they help teach children *how* to think about moral problems. However, they are far from enough. Much deeper changes—a change in the foundation of our entire conceptualizing will be necessary if we wish to survive.

These suggestions are only a small beginning. They indicate some of the directions we must take if we wish to lead our children to an ethical viewpoint that will help them survive the atomic and space age.

It will not be easy. The examples given of change in this paper are the kind of activities that are going on in only a very small percentage of our educational institutions. Seymour Sarason, in his important book, *The Culture of the School and the Problem of Change* has shown how difficult real change is in the schools. For reasons that Sarason describes in detail, there is a tremendous problem of inertia and a strong tendency to return to old patterns of "behavioral regularities" (patterns of recurrent behavior) in our educational systems.[17] Putting any new development in method into place is like swimming upstream in a rapidly flowing river. As soon as one stops swimming one is swept back to where one started from.

But, difficult or not, we must change. Eleanor Roosevelt once put it, "The whole future of our country depends on the education of our children."[18] It is now more than that. The whole future of our species depends on it.

ENDNOTES

Kohlberg, L. in Scarf, Peter (Ed.) Readings in Moral Education, Winston Press, Oak Grove, MN, 1978, p. 8.

[1] This originally was Hegel's criticism of Kantian philosophy.

The child's learning of right and wrong, an understanding which grows primarily out of the adult-child relationship, but is stabilized in practice with peers.... Children do need the chance to work things out for themselves; they need the struggle, the conflict and the tears to value the pleasures that come with satisfactory solutions...Lecturing is not effective. Cohn, D., The Learning Child, Pantheon, NY, 1972, p. 61.

Friedrich Froebel, who was largely responsible for originating modern education, stressed two concepts as the basis of what education should strive for. The first was the concept of self activity (Selbsttätigkeit). The second was the concept, in Froebel's language, of Gleidganzes, which roughly translates into "a whole that develops because it is, in turn, part of a larger whole—it is a participant whole."

In this book, as in the viewpoint of Susan Blow, a major figure in the development of the kindergarten movement in the United States, children's learning is seen as essentially social. They are understudies in the drama of history. They must learn their lines well before they can, as indeed they properly should, rewrite those lines themselves. Development...is an active interplay between the inner and the outer—the inner and the outer equally valued.

Dropkin, Ruth and Tobier, A. (Eds.) Roots of Open Education in America, The City College Workshop Center for Open Education, New York City, 1976, p. 52

In this approach you are concerned, like Aristotle, more with the practice than with the theory of morals. For him, to become a good person, you must behave like a good person. Then you will know what goodness is and be accustomed to living with it. This is quite different from the theoretical stance, from Plato to many educational groups in the present, who believed that first there must be the theoretical understanding of ethics and from this would follow ethical behavior.

In Aristotle's words:

...a person becomes just by the performance of just actions and temperate by the performance of temperate actions, nor is there the smallest likelihood of a person becoming good by any other course of conduct. This is not, however, a popular line to take, most people preferring theory to practice under the impression that arguing about morals proves them to be philosophers and that in this way they will turn out to be fine characters. Nichomachean Ethics, Book 2, Chapter 5.

The Ethics of Aristotle (J.A.K. Thomson, Tr.) Penguin,

Harmondsworth, Middlesex, 1955, p. 62
Clearly, of course, both theory and practice are needed. Theory without practice is weak and erratic. Practice without theory is blind action. See, for example, Clark, Gordon and Smith, T.V., Readings in Ethics, Appleton-Century-Crofts, New York, 1935, p. 6 ff.

[2] Lewis, Gertrude, Teach Us What We Want to Know, Mental Health Materials Center, New York City, 1969

[3] The educator, Ernest O. Melby has summed this up succinctly when he wrote:
[The present school system] thinks first of what the child must learn and second of the child. We do not measure what school subjects do to the child. We measure what the child does to the school subjects.
In Raubinger, F. and Rowe, H. (Eds.) The Individual and Education, Macmillan, New York, 1968, p. 3
The usual school system of marking on a curve is a good way of teaching students to compete rather than to cooperate. It has been called "the fang and claw" method of grading. And if you think about the implications to the student of multiple choice tests—such as that originality of thought makes you fail—the concept of the "hidden curriculum" becomes even more clear.
In the words of the educator Alice U. Kelliher, "Everything we do in a classroom tells loudly what we care about, what we value..." Talks with Teachers, Educational Publishing Corp., Darien, CT, 1958, p. 15

[4] These examples were described to me by the educator Lillian Weber.

[5] National Students Volunteer Program, Washington DC.

[6] Dickson, Alec, "Foreword" in Goodlad, Sinclair, Education and Social Action, Harper & Row, New York, 1975, p. 8

[7] Goodlad, S., op. cit., p. 142

[8] It is far past time to look carefully at our basic *attitudes* about education—what do we really believe is the purpose of our schools. Unless we do this, we are not going to make meaningful changes in a system that is largely failing by almost any standard. In this context, it may be helpful top recall that the first really heavy Federal money that came to our schools came, in the United States, after the Russians were the first into space. First came Sputnik and then the National Defense Education Act. As the President said at the time, education was important as it helped in our fight against our enemies.

[9] It seems to me perfectly clear that we can replace the agenda of the

19th Century's pious idealism by something much more exciting—something much more challenging, and certainly not something to be complacent about. We can say that, from here on out, there is going to be one central preoccupation for human beings, for which we must, as all costs, prepare ourselves. ...that is the task before us of becoming something that we have never really thought much about: becoming the custodians of this planet.

David Hawkins, "Developing a New Educational Agenda" in Dropkin and Tobier, p. 57.

The emphasis in this chapter has been on helping the child develop his or her relationships with themselves, others and with the environment. But more is needed in education. A child must also learn skills and content. Herbert Kohl, who understood deeply the importance of human and social growth of the student put it thus:

Teaching does not consist solely of making the youngsters feel good about themselves. It involves helping students gain understanding, knowledge and skills they didn't previously have.

Growing Minds, Harper & Row, New York, 1984, p. 89

[10] Starrett, Robert O., Sowing Seeds of Faith and Justice, Jesuit Secondary Education Association Publishers, Washington, DC, Undated

[11] Cohn, Dorothy, The Learning Child, Pantheon, New York, 1972, p. 2, 3, ff.

[12] Likona, Thomas, Educating for Character, Bantam, New York, 1991.

[13] Newman, Fred and Rutter, Robert, "A Profile of High School Community Service Projects. Educational Leadership, December 1985 and January 1986

[14] Newman, Fred W., Education for Citizen Action, McCutchan, Berkeley, CA, 1975

[15] Field, Kenneth and Kevin, John A., "Why Doesn't Everyone Work to Prevent Nuclear War?" Journal of Applied Psychology, 1988, Vol. 18, No. I., pp. 59-65

[16] For a fuller discussion of concepts in this Appendix, see LeShan, Eda J., The Conspiracy Against Childhood, Atheneum, New York, 1976, Helios, 2003

[17] Sarason, Seymour, The Culture of the School and the Problem of Change, Alleyn and Bacon, Inc., Boston, 1971

[18] Kelliher, A., Op. Cit., p. 3

CHAPTER 8

OUT OF PANDORA'S BOX

WE LIVE IN A terribly important time. In all likelihood, this century will determine the future of the human race. For the first time we have both the tools with which we can destroy ourselves and the tools with which we can save ourselves. In the hand that reaches toward the darkness we have atomic weapons, deliberately designed plagues and previously nonexistent chemical poisons,. Our new industrial abilities can easily and permanently ruin the delicate ecological balance of our only planet and leave us without breathable air or drinkable water. Our new medical abilities can easily lead to such overpopulation that all our genetically designed crops and green revolutions will still leave us starving.

These are not dire science fiction fantasies. They are as real as your house or car. In the hand that reaches toward the light we have the information and tools of the social sciences, our knowledge of the needs of children and the work of our parent educators, the history of such organizations as the Sierra Club and Greenpeace and The International Whaling Commission, and the experience of the United Nations and from Kyoto.

The 20th Century was the time of development of these tools for our move to the next step of the human race, the movement toward a patriotism toward the group that includes all members of our species. The 21st Century is the time we can put them together.

In the last few centuries we have made a scientific and industrial revolution that has opened Pandora's Box. Out of it has come a tremendous ability for good or for evil. The future can swing either way; it is balanced on a cusp.

Each of us has the ability to influence in which direction the world moves. And we do not have to join the Peace Corps or leave our homes and occupations to do this (although glory and our gratitude to those who can and do.) All we have to do is be aware of whom we vote for and what we buy and how we protect children. This has been the point of this book, that if each of us moves as individuals, a step at a time, we can have effects and set up positive currents for larger effects that will move us toward the light. The ancient truth is "If the leaders have no vision the people perish." The truth today is that is if the people, one by one, develop a vision, the leaders will follow and the people will survive.

SOME FURTHER THOUGHTS ON PATRIOTISM

THERE IS ALSO ANOTHER kind of work for the future that we can be involved in and still continue to fulfill the responsibilities we have to our family and our careers. This is to try to open our minds and to think beyond some of the basic assumptions built so deeply into our culture that we are hardly aware that they exist.

These are rarely questioned by anyone. It is very hard to think beyond the limits of the thoughts of the society in which we developed. Plato, one of the greatest minds of human history, could not envision a patriotism to a group larger than the city state in which Greek society existed during his lifetime. He saw the ideal society as made up of separate cities of about five thousand families each. He also, and ethical considerations were a major focus of his thought, could not envision a society that was not built on slavery. That these two concepts—the city state and the necessity of slavery—were basic and inexorable laws of nature was so firmly built into his culture that they were never questioned. Since his time, of course, they have been deeply questioned and then discarded.

There are some similar basic assumptions built into our own culture. These were acceptable, and often positive and helpful, in the past but are absolutely destructive to the future now. Can you begin the terribly difficult task of widening your mind to accept the fact that they exist? And after doing that the further task of beginning to question their validity today? The two most dangerous assumptions for the future, assumptions which have been hidden in plain sight from most of us, are:

1. Every person has the inalienable right to own as many goods, as many materials things, as he can honestly accumulate. This includes automobiles.

2. Every couple and every woman has a natural right to have as many children as they or she wishes or as whim or chance dictate.

There have been in the past "sumptuary laws"—laws on how much wealth you could display and estate taxes decreasing the amount you could pass on to your heirs. However, in Western society there have been no laws limiting the amount you could own or the number of children you could have.

These assumptions were acceptable in the past when production was slow and limited and when the death rate in childbirth and in childhood was so high. Since the scientific production and distribution revolution of the 19th Century and the medical revolutions of the late 1800s (the germ theory and the alliance with chemistry) this has changed. They have gone slowly from being benign to being malignant.

There is little question today that one of the greatest dangers that faces the human race, and one that is a terrible threat to the environment which we will leave to our children and their children, is one that is very little talked about. We all know that it is something that if unchecked will destroy us, yet it is never brought up in legislative halls and to raise the subject in social situations is considered gauche at best and quite boorish. This is the fact that our population is steadily, and with increasing speed, growing to the point that the Earth's resources (and standing room!) can not handle it. We can, and must put as many Band-Aids on the problem as we can with "green revolutions" and better methods of food production, but no matter how ingenious and clever we are with this sort of thing, underneath the superficial solutions, doom keeps advancing toward us.

(If you are a Westerner raised in the 20th Century, at this point look within and see what is your reaction to the preceding paragraphs. For most of us it is boredom or irritation. We tend strongly to turn away from this subject with something like, "Yes, that's true, and now let's go on to see what else they have to say." or "This is rather boring. I wonder what is on TV." or else just shut the book with a feeling or irritation. There is usually a sense that it is time to go to some other activity besides reading this inane and upsetting book. Check yourself at this time and most of us will get some sense of how deeply these assumptions are ingrained in our society and how they are accompanied by a sign that says "Keep Off, Avoid This Territory.")

We have not here included any statistics on the

population growth rate or dire predictions as to what
will happen if we do not take action. Writers far more
knowledgeable and skilled than we are have done this
to no noticeable effect. As examples Jonathan Schell
or Paul and Ann Erlich come to mind here. Rather I
want to stress that we have now an opportunity we
have never had before. With modern communication
all nations of the world have the same present. And
our children grow up playing and learning from the
internet which ignores all national boundaries. They
are ready for us to teach them that they are loved
because they see adults working for their safety and in
the future. And by involving them we can teach them
that they have the power to make meaningful changes
in the world. Together we can, in the poet William
Blake's words, work to "…build Jerusalem in England's
green and pleasant Land." And that goes not only for
Great Britain but for the rest of the world also.

There is another important assumption built into
our culture that often profoundly affects our thinking
and actions. It is rarely stated clearly or questioned
even though our actual experience demonstrates how
false and invalid it is. This is the belief that "happiness"
comes when we have fulfilled our needs and when no
"want" is pressing on us.

The philosopher John Dewey once pointed out
that there are two separate kinds of "retirement."
There is, he said, "Retirement From" and "Retirement
To." In the first one, Retirement From, the person has
worked at a job long and hard enough so that he or
she can stop working and know that the needs of food,

shelter, entertainment and so forth are taken care of and will not have to be worried about any more. There is no tension or anxiety about fulfilling these for the rest of one's life. There is nothing in particular that the person involved "needs" to do. Very often there has been a looking forward to this for many years. Without the stress of their occupation they expect to be "happy" and are looking forward to "travel," "golf," or "just doing nothing in particular."

Generally speaking this expectation is not fulfilled. Instead there is boredom, depression, irritation, and often despair.

A patient told one of us (LLL) that he loved to play golf and tennis and for many years had wished for nothing more than to be able to do them full time. When he finally retired still full of energy at sixty-five he knew that now he could fulfill this long time dream.

Two years later he was at St. Andrews—that Mecca for devoted golfers—with a very congenial group of friends. The weather was idyllic. They played golf all morning and tennis in the afternoons. As he lay in bed when he woke up on the sixth day he realized that he was hoping that today there would a rainstorm!

Retirement From is, statistically speaking, the greatest cause of death in our time. Very often the biological defenses of the body appear to begin to function at a much lower level than they did prior to stopping work and giving up one's occupation and the goals implied in its activities. The death rate from heart disease, cancer and all other major causes shows major increases in the five-year period following retirement no matter whether this is at the age of fifty-five, sixty,

sixty-five, seventy or later. Further we all know people who "retired from," after looking forward to it for years and who shortly after were bored, goalless and regretted the change.

Retirement To is quite different. In this the person leaves his previous and long-term occupation in order to be able to work at something he or she really wants to do. The new work is done for its own sake, not for a paycheck. Often it is volunteer work. Often the person works far harder at the new occupation than was done at the old one. The new work makes the person feel fulfilled, there is much more enthusiasm in their lives and when they are tired from working it is much more often the "good tired" feeling than it is the "dragged out" feeling. And they are far "happier."

Working in the way we have been describing in this book has another effect. There are a very large number of people in the Western world today who feel a sense of despair about the negative political and social developments they see around them. They feel helpless and that they can have no meaningful effect in changing things. So great is this feeling that the World Health Organization has predicted the most common illness by the year 2012 will be psychological depression. There are tens of millions who take Prozac or similar drugs to give back meaning to their lives. The very large number of children on substances like Ritalin is shocking and frightening.

We can not shield our inner life from the world we perceive around us. Like it or not we are connected to others of our species. There is a need to express this connection. So long as we devote our caring and concern only to ourselves, our immediate family, and perhaps to the company for which we work, something in us is unfulfilled. We are incomplete.

Part of the present book derives from a long term study by one of us (LLL) on how to help people with catastrophic illness stimulate their immune systems and bring the inner physician to the aid of the outer one.[1] It was found that dealing with physical factors (such as nutrition and exercise) and psychological factors (such as the usual kind of problem discussed in psychotherapy) helped considerably. However, far better results were obtained when people also became committed to some action for others on a larger scale. Becoming involved, often for the first time in their lives, in the kinds of action we have described in this book, in addition to working on the other levels, often increased the functioning of the self-healing mechanisms to a large degree. Very often startlingly similar remarks were made by different individuals who had done this along the line of, "It fed a part of me I did not know was there and certainly did not know was hungry!" A little known but important book for psychotherapists demonstrates that this approach when added to more standard methods of psychotherapy markedly improves the results.[2]

We are a social species with all that this implies. Our inner life functions far better when we accept this fact, and act on the acceptance, that we are "involved in mankind." John Gardner wrote, out of his long experience in public service:

> *The experience of recent years suggests that the service idea, as exemplified in The Peace Corps and VISTA, taps a rich vein of motivation....When people are serving life is no longer meaningless. They no longer*

feel rootless. They feel responsible.[3]

If we look back into our lives with as few preconceptions as we can manage and ask ourselves not when we were "happiest" but what periods we would most like to repeat we will usually find that these are periods when we worked hard for long hours for something we believed to be very worthwhile. There were times when we had a goal and threw ourselves into trying to attain it. This is the true definition of "happiness" for human beings. Not freedom from tension and need, but an orientation to something believed to be of value and circumstances permitting us to work long and hard toward its achievement. And it is in these periods that we feel ourselves to be most ourselves and to be living the life we were built for.

In 1878 the philosopher and psychologist William James wrote a letter to a friend.

I have often thought that the best way to define a man's character would be to seek out the particular mental and moral attitude which, when it came upon him, he felt himself most deeply and intensely active and alive...at such moments there is a voice inside which says "This is the real me!"

If we look at our own experience we will find that the moments James describes are in periods that fit the definition of "happiness" we have described above.

If we want to help our children to grow up to a life of enthusiasm and personal fulfillment we must teach them that there are worthwhile goals toward which they can work. We do this best by example and if we choose patriotic goals—patriotic in the sense that this book is defining—we will not only help to enhance their lives (and our own!) but will likely set up ripple effects that will help our culture move in the direction we hope for for our children and their children.

The viewpoint of this section was expressed in slightly other terms by one of us (EJL) over fifteen years ago in her column in Newsday and reprinted in her book *I Want More of Everything* (Newmarket Press, New York 1994).

Retirement: From or To?

The Richardsons came for lunch: friends we hadn't seen for twenty years since we both moved from place to place. It was obvious from the expression on their faces that they were as relieved as we were to see, at once, we still liked each other and had common interests. Except for one unbridgeable sad area. Helen and Martin had owned and worked together in a very fine women's clothing shop. Martin did the buying, Helen the selling; both loved their work. Without having had any children they could devote themselves to attending fashion shows all over the world, met many designers, and had devoted customers for thirty years. Having some mistaken notion they were getting too old and should retire and "enjoy themselves," they sold the business ten years ago.

During lunch, Larry and I realized we were dealing with two seriously depressed people, in excellent health but with no place to go. When Larry asked Helen what she'd been doing, she replied bitterly, "Who has anything to do?" Martin said sadly he was sorry he gave up tennis ten years ago; if he'd kept it up he could still play. Martin and Helen spend most of their time traveling, mainly to places they have been to before—because, "I guess we've just about seen everything twice already." We should have told Martin to try tennis again, slowly, carefully. We should have told Helen to get the lead out and do something useful.

We were embarrassed to indicate we were still so busy that we couldn't see straight. They seemed genuinely shocked that we had no plans to retire at seventy-one and seventy-four. Martin tells dirty jokes, which he never did before, and Helen seems to have given up things I remember she enjoyed once, such as cooking and reading and listening to music.

We reminisced about old times and Helen said she hoped it wouldn't be another twenty years, and I thought to myself, it can't be.

After they left, Larry, the family intellectual, recited these lines from a poem by Tennyson about the aged Ulysses getting ready to lead his old friends on a new, and possibly final, adventure:

> *Old Age hath yet his honor and his toil;*
> *Death closes all; but something ere the end,*
> *Some work of noble note may yet be done..."*

And I told Larry I had just heard about a seventy-eight-year-old women, with no family left, who was planning to cross from Newfoundland to Europe alone in a sailboat. Some of her friends wondered if she should be placed in a mental hospital, but her answer seemed quite sane to me. "If I die gloriously happy, would that be so bad? And if I can't do what I want now, when may I start?"

It's a tragedy to retire from something we love unless we are ready to fall in love with something new.

Another aspect of this is present in another article reprinted in the book by EJL *It's Better to be Over the Hill Than Under It* (Newmarket Press, New York, 1990).

Dealing with the Retirement Blues

I met a woman who is sixty-two years old and could now retire on an excellent pension. Her husband retired two years ago, and wants his wife to retire so they can both be free to travel and develop new interests—perhaps take some courses, be able to join a health club, and so on.

Millie couldn't explain why she was hesitant to retire. She told me she hated her job and had felt that way for twenty years. She had been struggling desperately to help people in trouble but the bureaucracy for which we worked had long since broken her spirit. "How can I retire," she asked me, "when I feel as if my life has been meaningless?"

I had heard many reasons why people hesitated to retire—fear of financial insecurity, loving one's work, no ideas or plans for things one might want to do, tedium, boredom—but I had never heard of someone unable to retire because of feelings of failure, of having wasted one's life. But the minute I heard the explanation I knew it was very likely to have been an unconscious feeling for many people who are unable to face that hidden agenda.

The more I thought about it the more it seemed to me that even if it might be very painful to retire on a note of triumph, it would be far more difficult to leave on a note of despair about one's life work.

Facing that sense of failure, not to have lived (and worked) as creatively as possible, need not mean a terrible ending. After acceptance and grief there can, of course, be a new beginning. If one's work was hateful and even useless, is that the end of the road? Quite the opposite. This is the moment for asking the question, "What kind of work would I do if I were starting all over?" By the nature of things we started working when we were very young and probably didn't know much about ourselves. By the time we are in our sixties, life has taught us more about who we are; we have unearthed wishes, dreams, and talents we didn't even suspect we had when we were in our twenties. What a great opportunity for reassessment now! I cannot think of any dream that cannot be fulfilled in some fashion in the later years. Maybe we now know we always wanted to become a buyer in a large department store; isn't there a small boutique or dress shop in the neighborhood that needs a part-time salesperson? Maybe, after thirty years as a secretary, you know you should have become a nursery-school teacher. I cannot believe there is a daycare center anywhere in the country that doesn't need volunteers. Maybe you wished that you could have an effect on the world on a larger scale. Volunteers are needed by the Natural Resources Defense Council, by Amnesty International and many others. Try, for example one of the supporting organizations for Shaare Zedek Hospital in Jerusalem (where they do not care what a patient's race or religion is and no one is ever turned away for lack of funds) or the Quaker Relief Fund or Catholic Charities or—just ask your local librarian to continue the list. Maybe you became a teacher or a lawyer, when what you wish you'd done was write musicals for the theater. Now is the chance to be a "gofer" for an off-Broadway or summer theater, or take courses in theater arts, or help kids put on plays in a community center. Dreams can't be rigid and inflexible, but with clever modifications and adjustments we can find activities that we've never allowed ourselves to try before.

I always thought that depression on retirement had to do most often with missing work. Now I think some of that depression may be the thought, "I never really lived." If that's the case it is never too late to start a new life, if we relinquish the past and use our imagination.

ENDNOTES

[1] See, for example, LeShan, L., Cancer as a Turning Point, New York, Penguin, 1990, Plume, 1994, or www.cancerasaturning point.org.

[2] Porter, Kenneth, Rinzler, Deborah and Olsen, Paul, Heal or Die: Psychotherapists Confront Nuclear Annihilation, New York, Psychohistory Press, 1987.

[3] Gardner, John W., The Recovery of Confidence, New York, Pocket Books, 1971, p. 52.